Collins
SCOTTISH
PLACE NAMES

Collins

HarperCollins Publishers
Westerhill Road
Bishopbriggs
Glasgow
G64 2QT

www.collinslanguage.com

First Edition 2009

ISBN 978-0-00-729947-8

Text © John Abernethy 2009

Illustrations © Alex Collier 2009

The moral rights of the author
have been asserted

The moral rights of the illustrator
have been asserted

Collins® is a registered
trademark of HarperCollins
Publishers Limited

A catalogue record for this book
is available from the British
Library.

Designed and typeset by
Thomas Callan

Printed in Great Britain by
Clays Ltd, St Ives plc

Author's Note

The list of names covered in this book is by no means an exhaustive or comprehensive list of all the places in Scotland, but is intended to be an alphabetical compendium of the most interesting and important ones.

In many cases a definitive explanation for the meaning of the name has been lost in time (rivers in particular are of especially ancient origin) and the definitions given in this book are the ones generally considered to be the most likely, although in many cases the meanings are still disputed. Wherever possible I have mentioned alternative suggestions as to the origin of a place name.

The subject of Scottish place names is a truly fascinating one, and I would recommend that anyone who enjoys this book pursues further reading and research to gain a greater understanding of the country.

Introduction

Scotland is home to some truly fantastic place names. These range from the quintessentially Scottish (Auchtermuchty, Kirkintilloch, Drumnadrochit) to the romantic (Skye and Iona) and even the monosyllab ically direct (Rum, Ayr, Cults). Some Scottish places have proved popular as first names (Lewis, Angus, Kyle), while others have been successful international exports (Dallas, Perth, Hamilton). Then again, some come across as being downright bewildering: why is Milngavie pronounced as though it were written 'Millguy' and Strathaven as though it were 'Straven'?

Many Scots identify themselves as being from the place where they were born or the place where they live, but how many actually know what that name means or where it came from?

The history of Scottish place names is as fascinating as the history of Scotland itself, and indeed the two subjects are inextricably intertwined. Scotland has been settled by Celts, Britons, Picts, Angles, Irish, Vikings, Normans, and English (amongst others) and the place names of Scotland mirror that diverse heritage. The two largest cities in Scotland, Glasgow and Edinburgh, are considered throughout the world as personifications of Scottishness, yet these places come from completely different linguistic traditions – Glasgow from old Celtic Brythonic (the southern branch of Celtic languages) and Edinburgh from Old English. Even the name 'Scotland' itself is formed by tacking the English word *land* on to the Latin *Scotti*, a word with the rather uncomplimentary meaning of 'pirates', which was given to the Irish people who settled in the west of Scotland around AD500 and would later give their name to an entire nation.

So we have ancient Celtic names for Scotland's great rivers – the Clyde, the Forth, the Tay – so old that nobody knows their true meanings, and the Brythonic influence remained in Strathclyde, which remained a separate kingdom until 1018. We also have some surviving Pictish names (although far less than you might imagine, due to the scarcity of Pictish written records which disappear from Scottish history from around AD900).

There is a smorgasbord of Scandinavian names in places ranging from Dumfries and Galloway in the south to the Hebrides in the west and right up to Orkney and Shetland in the far north. This Scandinavian influence is a reminder of the rule of the Norsemen from the 10th century right through to 1469 when the King of Denmark donated Orkney and Shetland to Scotland as a rather unusual wedding dowry for his daughter.

Then, of course, there is the Gaelic tradition. Gaelic was the national language of all of Scotland north of the Forth and Clyde until the 11th century, and it remained the national language of half of Scotland until the depopulation that began to take place in the Highlands and Islands from the 18th century onwards.

And finally we have the English tradition found in Lothian and the Borders. These areas were never Gaelic speaking and were only absorbed into the Scottish nation in 1034, bringing with them a language that would eventually take over the rest of the country. English became the language of the Scottish court in the reign of Malcolm III and Queen Margaret in the 11th century. The united Scottish nation began to use the English name of 'Scotland' rather than the Gaelic name of 'Alba' and the people of the Lowlands of Scotland began to speak their own version of English – Scots.

Within this linguistic melting pot the population of Scotland grew. New villages and towns were built and were given names that derived from Gaelic or Norse or Scots or sometimes a combination of different languages. Many place names have very straightforward origins – a field here, a church there, a hill next to the burn – but for every 'church by the hill' there are several Scottish place names whose origins are the subject of much academic debate and which prompt numerous theories about what came first, the Muck or the Eigg.

In *Scottish Place Names* we take you on a tour of Scotland from the Scandinavian-influenced Northern Isles to the Gaelic-speaking Western Isles, through the mighty mountain ranges and stunning lochs of the Highlands to the historic burghs and industrial towns of the Lowlands. It is a fascinating journey of many languages and cultures, of a country of incomers and invaders, a country of battle, a country of religion, and a country of quite a few steep hills.

Aberdeen

City in the north-east of Scotland, the third-largest city in the country. Aberdeen was one of the first of Scotland's royal burghs in the 12th century, and today is the busiest and wealthiest port in Britain. Aberdeen University was established in 1495 and is one of two universities in Aberdeen (the other being The Robert Gordon University).

The name 'Aberdeen' may be a combination of the old Brythonic word *aber* meaning 'where waters meet' or 'the mouth of the river' and *deen* which refers to the River Dee, or else it may come from the old world *Aberdon* ('where the River Don meets the sea') or from *Aberdoen* ('where the Rivers Dee and Don meet each other'). Or perhaps it is from some combination of the three.

Aberdeen is also known as 'The Granite City' as many of Aberdeen's buildings were built with local granite, giving the city that welcoming grey look, and 'Europe's Oil Capital' due to the impact of North Sea Oil from the 1970s onwards. A more jocular nickname is 'Furryboots City', because the question 'where are you from?' when asked in the Aberdonian dialect becomes 'Furryboots ye fae?'

Before the advent of oil, Aberdeen was famous for being Scotland's main fishing port. Trawling for white fish began there in 1882. The popular song

1

'The Northern Lights of Old Aberdeen' refers to the atmospheric phenomenon known as the Aurora Borealis rather than to Aberdeen's vibrant nightlife.

Aberdeen is famous for its local butteries called 'rowies', for its local newspaper *The Press and Journal* (noted for its sometimes parochial viewpoint, as in the apocryphal story of its greeting the sinking of *The Titanic* with the line 'Aberdeen Man Feared Lost'), and for being the home of Aberdeen Football Club, where in the 1980s Alex Ferguson made his name on the way to becoming the dominant force in British football management.

Residents of Aberdeen are called Aberdonians. Famous Aberdonians include missionary Mary Slessor, footballer Denis Law, ex-Goodie and *I'm Sorry I Haven't a Clue* stalwart Graeme Garden, and singer Annie Lennox of The Eurythmics, who sang 'Here Comes the Rain Again' (presumably thinking about her home city). The 4th Earl of Aberdeen, George Hamilton-Gordon was British Prime Minister from 1852 to 1855 but resigned after the mismanagement of the Crimean War.

There is another Aberdeen in Washington State, USA, that was the birthplace of Kurt Cobain of Nirvana. Aberdeen is also the name of a famous harbour on the south of Hong Kong Island.

Aberdeen Angus cattle are black beef cattle without

horns that were originally bred in Aberdeenshire and Angus.

Aberfeldy

Picturesque town on the River Tay in Perthshire. 'The Birks of Aberfeldy' is the name of a poem by Robert Burns, and famous people born in Aberfeldy include actor Alan Cumming. The name 'Aberfeldy' derives from the Brythonic *aber* meaning 'where waters meet' and the nearby stream called Pheallaig Burn.

Aberfoyle

Village in the Loch Lomond and the Trossachs National Park, popular tourist destination and known as 'The Gateway to the Trossachs'. Aberfoyle is associated with the famous outlaw Rob Roy Macgregor, who lived in the area, and the name 'Aberfoyle' derives from the Brythonic *aber* meaning 'where the waters meet' and the Gaelic *phuill* meaning 'pool'.

Abernethy

The name of both a village in Perthshire and a Highland forest. The Perthshire Abernethy is the location of an 11th-century round tower and was a major centre and possibly the capital of the Pictish kingdom. The Highland Abernethy Forest is in the Cairngorms National Park and has Nethy Bridge as its main village.

The name 'Abernethy' means 'mouth of the River Nethy' and derives from the Brythonic *aber* meaning 'mouth of' or 'where the waters meet' with the word 'Nethy' being of ancient origin and possibly meaning 'glistening'. The Abernethy in Perthshire is not, however, located near the River Nethy, and it might possibly be named after Nechtan, an 8th-century Pictish king.

Abernethy has also become a Scottish surname best known for the Abernethy biscuit that was invented in the 19th century by Dr John Abernethy (no relation to the author, as far as I know).

Aboyne

Small town on the River Dee in Aberdeenshire and home of the Aboyne Highland Games. The name 'Aboyne' possibly derives from the Gaelic words *ath* meaning 'ford' and *boinne* meaning 'rippling water'.

Airdrie

Town in North Lanarkshire that grew in the 19th century through the coal and iron industries. The name comes from the Gaelic *airde ruighe* meaning 'high hill slope'.

Alexandria

Largest town in the Vale of Leven in West Dunbartonshire. Alexandria lies on the River Leven and was a former industrial town. Alexandria is not named after the historic city of Alexandria in Egypt, but was named after the then local Member of Parliament, Alexander Smollett, possibly proving that politicians were more highly thought of in the 18th century than they are today.

Alloa

Administrative centre of Clackmannanshire on the north bank of the River Forth. Alloa used to be a major Scottish brewing town and its name comes from the Gaelic *ailmagh* meaning 'rocky plain'.

Alloway

Ayrshire village that is now a suburb of Ayr. Alloway is best known for being the birthplace, in 1759, of a certain Robert Burns who later went on to achieve some fame as a poet. The place where he was born, Burns Cottage, is a popular tourist destination. Alloway was the setting for Burns' most famous poem, *Tam o' Shanter*, which features the Old Kirk of Alloway where the witches and warlocks dance and the Brig o' Doon where Tam's horse has his tail pulled off.

Brig o' Doon would later inspire the famous American musical and film *Brigadoon*, which tells the story of a magical Scottish village that only appears once a year.

The origin of the name 'Alloway' is believed to have more in common with 'Alloa' than with 'Galloway' and means 'rocky plain', coming from the Gaelic word *ailmagh*.

Angus

Local-government authority in the East of Scotland. Angus was historically claimed to be one of the original seven 'mormaerdoms' or minor kingdoms of Scotland dating back to the 10th century. The region is said to take its name from the 8th-century Pictish king Aonghus (or Oengus) whose name meant 'unique choice' and was also the name of a Celtic god.

The cattle known in Britain by the name 'Aberdeen Angus' are usually called 'Angus cattle' in the United States. Angus is both a popular Scottish surname and male first name, with the most famous owner of the name probably being guitarist Angus Young of the Australian rock band AC/DC.

Annan

Town and river in south-west Scotland. The origin of the name is unknown, although it has been suggested that it simply derives from an old Brythonic name for 'water'. Famous people born in Annan include *Ugly Betty* star Ashley Jensen, but former UN Secretary-General Kofi Annan has no known connection with the town.

The area around Annan is known as Annandale and was where a certain Bruce family were given land and the title of Lord of Annandale in the 13th century before becoming the royal family of Scotland.

Antonine Wall

Roman fortified wall that crosses Scotland from Old Kilpatrick on the Firth of Clyde to near Bo'ness on the Firth of Forth. The Antonine Wall is 37 miles long and is mainly built of turf on stone foundations. Surviving parts can be seen at Bearsden, Kilsyth, and Falkirk, and the Wall is now a World Heritage Site. The Antonine Wall is the most important reminder of the short-lived Roman occupation of Scotland (the longer Hadrian's Wall being located in what is now Northern England). The Wall was built around AD142 and was abandoned at some time in the 160s. It is named after the Roman emperor Antoninus Pius, the adopted son and successor of Hadrian, who ruled from 138 to 161.

Anstruther

Popular coastal town and former major fishing port in the East Neuk of Fife. Famous people born in Anstruther include Thomas Chalmers, the first Moderator of the Free Church of Scotland (or 'Wee Frees') and Radio 1 DJ Edith Bowman. The name 'Anstruther' derives from the Gaelic *an sruthair* meaning 'the little stream', although locally the town is known as 'Ainster'.

Appin

Mountainous area of Argyll and formerly a stronghold of the Stewart Clan. Appin is perhaps best known for the 16th-century Castle Stalker built on an islet at Loch Laoich and for the Appin Murder of Colin Campbell, 'The Red Fox', in 1752. This murder, probably perpetrated by a Stewart, provided one of the major plotlines of Robert Louis Stevenson's novel *Kidnapped*. The name 'Appin' derives from the Gaelic *apuinn* meaning 'abbey land' in reference to a monastery on the nearby Isle of Lismore.

Arbroath

Historic town and port in Angus. Arbroath is famous for the Declaration of Arbroath, the most important document in Scotland's history, which stated the right of the people of Scotland to independence. The declaration was drafted in support of King Robert the Bruce at Arbroath Abbey on 6th April 1320, with its most famous line being (translated from the original Latin) 'For, as long as but a hundred of us remain alive, never will we on any conditions be brought under English rule.'

On Christmas Day 1950, the Stone of Destiny (traditionally used at the coronation of Scottish monarchs) was audaciously removed from Westminster Abbey. Its captors eventually deposited the stone at Arbroath Abbey (after a spot of repair work to repair the damage incurred during the incident) to mark the importance of this place in Scottish history.

To those with a taste for culinary rather than historical matters, however, Arbroath is famous for the 'Arbroath Smokie', a salted and hot smoked haddock.

Arbroath was originally a Pictish town with name of Aberbrothock, derived from the Brythonic word *aber* meaning 'mouth of' and *Brothock* the name of local burn that ran into the sea. In Gaelic, *Brothock* becomes *Brothach*, which also means 'turbulent', and the name 'Arbroath' derives from the Gaelic form.

Ardnamurchan

Peninsula in the north-west Highlands, known for its unspoilt beauty. Ardnamurchan Point, at the tip of the peninsula, has the distinction of being the most westerly point of both the Scottish and British mainland. There is some dispute about the meaning of 'Ardnamurchan': *ard* comes from the Gaelic *airde* meaning 'point' or 'peninsula', but *nam murchan* may mean either 'of the great seas' or 'of the otters'.

Argyll

Region on the west coast of mainland Scotland. Argyll was the name of a historical county of Scotland which has now been divided into two, with northern Argyll in the Highland region and the southern part forming the local-government area of Argyll and Bute. The region of Argyll is geographically similar to the ancient kingdom of Dalriada, established between the 6th and 9th centuries by the 'Scotti' who had emigrated from Ireland and would eventually give their name to the entire nation.

Argyll is long associated with the Campbell clan, for long the most powerful family in Scotland, and the head of the Argyll Campbells is also the chief of the Clan Campbell. Since 1701 the clan chief has also been given the title of Duke of Argyll.

The name 'Argyll' originates from the Gaelic *airer Gaidheal* and means 'coastland of the Gaels'. Argyll is sometimes spelt 'Argyle', as in Argyle Street, one of the most famous streets in Glasgow.

The Argyllshire Highlanders were a Campbell regiment, originally raised in 1794, but better known as the Argyll and Sutherland Highlanders from 1881.

Ardrossan

Town and port on the North Ayrshire coast. Ardrossan is best known as the place where you catch the ferry to sail to the island of Arran. The name 'Ardrossan' perhaps derives from the Gaelic *airde ros an* with *airde* meaning 'height', *ros* meaning 'headland' or 'promontory', and *an* meaning 'little'.

Arran

Island off the Ayrshire coast. A popular tourist destination, with aspects resembling both the Lowlands and the Highlands, Arran has been described as being 'Scotland in Miniature'.

Arran takes its name from the Gaelic *Arainn* or Brythonic *Aran*, both of which mean 'place of high peaks'. Arran has also in recent years joined the likes of Lewis, Harris, Skye, and Iona as one of the Scottish place names that is also a popular first name.

Arthur's Seat

Hill in Edinburgh. At 823 feet high, Arthur's Seat is
the highest peak in Holyrood Park, only a mile from
Edinburgh's city centre and popular with tourists
and walkers. The name 'Arthur's Seat' has been used
since at least the 15th century and is assumed to
be in honour of the legendary Celtic King Arthur
of Camelot, although it is possible that it might be
named after some other Arthur. From a distance, the
hill is said to resemble a crouching lion.

Assynt

Mountainous and remote coastal area in west
Sutherland and name of a loch in the same area. The
name 'Assynt' may derive from the Norse *ass* meaning
'rocky', thus making Assynt mean 'rocky area'.

Atholl

Ancient region of Scotland in what is now Perthshire.
Atholl was one of Scotland's earliest mormaerdoms
and later became an earldom. It was originally a
Stewart heartland before the title of Earl transferred to
the Murrays in 1629. In 1703 it became a dukedom
with Blair Castle, near Blair Atholl, the family seat.
The name 'Atholl' derives from the Gaelic *ath fhodla*
and means 'new Ireland'.

The Atholl Highlanders are a historic regiment first raised by the Duke of Atholl in the 18th century and continue today as the only private army in Britain. An 'Atholl Brose' is a famous Scottish delicacy consisting of honey, whisky, and oatmeal.

Auchtermuchty

Small town in Fife. One of the best-known place names in Scotland on account of its rich comic value, 'Auchtermuchty' derives from the Gaelic *uachdar* meaning 'high ground' and *muc garadh* meaning 'pig enclosure'. Famous people from Auchtermuchty include Craig and Charlie Reid, better known as The Proclaimers, and legendary accordionist Jimmy Shand, better known as the leader of Jimmy Shand and his Band.

Aviemore

Town and tourist destination in the Cairngorm range. Aviemore was developed in the 1960s to become Scotland's first centre for winter sports, although continued lack of snow has understandably proved a problem for a place attempting to establish itself as a premier skiing resort. The name derives from the Gaelic *agaidh* meaning 'pass' and *mor* meaning 'big' and is therefore 'big pass'.

Ayr

Town and port on the west coast of Scotland. Ayr has been a royal burgh since the 13th century and is well known for tourism, horse-racing (Ayr racecourse being the home of the Scottish Grand National), and through its connections to Robert Burns, who was born only two miles away in the village of Alloway. Burns once wrote of the people of Ayr in the epic poem *Tam o' Shanter*:

> *Auld Ayr wham ne'ar a toun surpasses*
> *For honest men and bonnie lassies*

… and Burns certainly knew quite a few of the latter.

Other famous people from Ayr include engineer John Loudon McAdam, who revolutionized road building with what would be named 'tarmacadam' in his honour.

Ayr took its name from the River Ayr at whose mouth the town was built. The origin of the name is unknown, although it is almost certainly of Brythonic origin.

Ayrshire is the greater region around Ayr and is divided into three local-government authorities: East Ayrshire, North Ayrshire and South Ayrshire. Much of Ayrshire is farming country and the Ayrshire is a breed of dairy cattle.

Badenoch

Historic and mountainous area of the Highlands along the River Spey. The name 'Badenoch' derives from the Gaelic *baithe* meaning 'flooded' and *ach* meaning 'land'. Alexander Stewart, Lord of Badenoch, was a famous and much feared 14th-century Scottish warlord whose ruthlessness earned him the soubriquet 'The Wolf of Badenoch'.

Ballater

Town in Aberdeenshire on the River Dee. Ballater was originally a spa town before becoming associated with the royal family from the 19th century onwards. As the nearest town to Balmoral it has become one of the most popular tourist destinations in Royal Deeside. The origins of the word 'Ballater' are not certain, although the name could derive from the Gaelic word *bealach* meaning 'mountain pass'. Famous people born in Ballater include pioneering town planner Patrick Geddes.

Balloch

Name of several villages in Scotland, notably one on the shore of Loch Lomond in West Dunbartonshire and one near Inverness. The Loch Lomond Balloch is a popular tourist destination and centre for the

Loch Lomond and Trossachs National Park. 'Balloch' derives from the Gaelic *bealach* and means 'mountain pass'.

Balmoral

Castle and estate on the River Dee. Balmoral was bought by Queen Victoria and Prince Albert in 1852 and became Victoria's private retreat and has remained in the ownership of the royal family to this day, forming the heart of the area known as Royal Deeside, where the Queen, Prince Philip, and the corgis spend their summer holidays. The origin of the name 'Balmoral' is unclear with *bal* deriving from the Gaelic *baile* meaning 'settlement' or 'farm' and *moral* perhaps deriving from the Gaelic *morail* meaning 'splendid'.

Balquhidder

Small village in Stirling, best known for being the home and burial place of the outlaw Rob Roy Macgregor. The name 'Balquhidder' is thought to derive from the Gaelic *baile* meaning 'settlement' or 'farm' and *chuil-tir* meaning 'distant'.

Banchory

Town on the River Dee. Banchory has become a commuter town serving Aberdeen and is often called 'The Gateway to Royal Deeside'. The name 'Banchory' is of disputed origin: it is suggested that it either derives from the Gaelic *beannach* meaning 'forked' (in reference to its location on the River Dee) or else from the Gaelic *beannchar* meaning 'blessed place' as a reference to the 6th-centrury Saint Ternan who is said to have brought Christianity to the region. Indeed, until relatively recent times the town was called Banchory Ternan.

Banff

Town on the north-east coast of Scotland. The town of Banff dates back at least to the 12th century, and its name either derives from the Gaelic *banbh* or *banbha* and could mean either 'land left fallow', 'a stream', or 'a pig'. The name of Banff and Buchan has recently become famous for being the long-standing parliamentary constituency of Scotland's First Minister, Alex Salmond, a man who has no doubt enjoyed an occasional bacon roll in his time.

Banff is also the name of a resort town in Alberta's Rocky Mountains, and the Canadian Banff now has a larger population than the Scottish town after which it was named.

Bannockburn

Village that is now a suburb of Stirling. Bannockburn was the site of the most famous battle ever fought on Scottish soil (and one of the few that Scotland actually won) when, on the 23rd and 24th of June 1314, the army of Robert the Bruce sent the English army of Edward II homewards to think again. There is a National Trust visitor centre and large statue of the Bruce at Bannockburn, but no one is quite sure of the actual location of the battlefield.

The name 'Bannockburn' originates in the Bannock, a stream that enters the River Forth close to the battlefield, and is possibly of Brythonic origin, but of unknown meaning. The Scots word *burn* meaning 'stream' was added later, probably after the battle.

The Scottish culinary delicacy called the bannock shares the same spelling and pronunciation as the Bannock Burn, but appears to be otherwise unconnected.

Barra

Island in the south of the Outer Hebrides. Noted for its natural beauty, Barra was the stronghold of the Clan MacNeill and is predominantly Catholic. The 1949 film *Whisky Galore* was shot on Barra, and Compton Mackenzie, the author of the book on which the film was based, is buried on the island. The island's airstrip is famous for being one of the very few public airstrips in the world where the plane lands on a beach.

The name 'Barra' possibly originates from the 6th-century Irish saint Finbarr, the patron saint of Cork, who is said to have preached on Barra. The name 'Finbarr' means 'white-haired' and with the addition of the Norse *ey* meaning 'island', this would make Barra 'hair island', although it is possible that Barra was so named even before the Vikings arrived.

Barrhead

Town in East Renfrewshire near Paisley. Barrhead became known for the manufacture of textiles and toilets. The name is thought to be Scots in origin, with *barr* being Scots for 'ploughed furrows' (rather than coming from the Gaelic word *barr* meaning 'hilltop'), and the original settlement of Barrhead was built at the head of the ploughed fields. Famous people born in Barrhead include Scottish footballer and manager Alex McLeish.

Bathgate

Industrial town in West Lothian. The name 'Bathgate' does not derive from either a bath or a gate, but from the Brythonic *baedd coed* meaning 'boar wood', harking back to a time when boars lived locally. Famous people born in Bathgate include pioneering doctor James Simpson, *Doctor Who* actor David Tennant, and motor racing driver Dario Franchitti.

Bearsden

Suburban town north-west of Glasgow in East Dunbartonshire. Bearsden is built on the site of the Antonine Wall with several sections of the Wall still visible today. Bearsden was previously called first New Kilpatrick and then New Kirk, before the building of today's town began in the 19th century. The current name was taken from the local railway station, which was in turn named after a nearby house, although it is unclear what the original significance of the name might have been. There is certainly little evidence of bears in this prosperous area.

Beauly

Highland town west of Inverness. The name 'Beauly' is French in origin, coming from the 13th-century Beauly Priory that was founded by French monks who gave it the name of *beau lieu* ('beautiful place').

The Beauly Firth is the inlet of the sea that goes from Beauly in the west to Inverness in the east where it enters the Moray Firth.

Bellshill

Town in North Lanarkshire and commuter town
serving Glasgow. The town was first called Bellshill in
the 19th century and was built on a hill on the site of
a village formerly known as Bellmill, after a Mr Bell
who owned a stone quarry there. Famous people born
in Bellshill include Labour politician Robin Cook,
singer Sheena Easton, and footballer Ally McCoist.

Benbecula

Hebridean island that lies between North and South
Uist and which is connected to both by causeways.
Benbecula has a population of over a 1000 people
and is predominantly Catholic and Gaelic-speaking.
There is much debate about the origin of the name
'Benbecula'. The island's Gaelic name *Beinn na
Faoghla* means 'mountain of the fords', although as the
island is essentially flat, it has been suggested that the
Beinn part of the name might be a mistranslation of a
more appropriate old Gaelic or Norse word.

Ben Lomond

Mountain on the east shore of Loch Lomond. Ben
Lomond is the most southerly of Scotland's Munros
(peaks over 3000 feet high), and is popular with hill-
walkers. The meaning of 'Lomond' is the same as in

'Loch Lomond' and possibly means 'beacon', thus making Ben Lomond 'beacon mountain'.

Ben Macdui

Mountain in the Cairngorm range. Ben Macdui is the highest peak in the Cairngorms and the second highest mountain in both Scotland and Britain. The name 'Macdui' is of uncertain origin but is said to be the Gaelic for 'the hill of the black pig' (as it is said that the mountain resembles a pig) rather than referring to the Clan MacDuff, who have the Gaelic name *MacDhuibh*.

Until the 19th century, when scientific precision was brought to the measuring of mountain heights, it was thought that Ben Macdui was actually higher than Ben Nevis, and it is in fact only 35 metres shorter. The 'Big Grey Man of Ben Macdui' is said to be either a giant ghost or yeti who lives on the mountain.

Ben Nevis

Mountain rising above Glen Nevis in Lochaber. Ben Nevis is the highest and best-known mountain in both Scotland and Britain at 4,409 feet. Despite, or probably because of, its great height, 100,000 people reach the summit every year, most following the popular 1883 Pony Track to the top.

'Ben' is the first name of most of Scotland's highest peaks and comes from the Gaelic *beinn* meaning 'mountain'. The word 'Nevis' has a disputed origin, deriving from the Gaelic name *Nibheis* it has been suggested as meaning either 'in the clouds' or 'venomous'.

Berwick

Historic town on the River Tweed. In the 12th and 13th centuries Berwick-upon-Tweed was a major trading port and one of the most important and wealthiest towns in Scotland. Its strategic position on the border of England and Scotland saw it repeatedly attacked by both countries and it changed hands a dozen times before finally being claimed by England in 1482.

Although Berwick-upon-Tweed has long been part of the England, Berwickshire remained in Scotland and was a historic county until becoming part of the Borders region in 1975.

The name 'Berwick' derives from the Old English *bere* meaning 'barley' and *wic* meaning 'farm'. Berwick-upon-Tweed is sometimes known to Scots as 'South Berwick' to differentiate it from the East Lothian town of North Berwick.

The football team from Berwick-upon-Tweed is called

Berwick Rangers and plays in the Scottish rather than the English league. The team is known as 'the wee Rangers' and defeated the more famous Rangers in the Scottish Cup in 1967.

Biggar

Historic market town in South Lanarkshire. The name might derive from the Norse *bygg* meaning 'barley' and *gardr* meaning 'field'. The town of Biggar gave its name to the surname Biggar and in turn became the subject of the tongue-twisting question 'Mrs Biggar had a baby boy. Who was bigger – Mrs Biggar or her baby?' The answer, of course, being the baby, as he was 'a little Biggar'.

Bishopbriggs

Town in East Dunbartonshire. Bishopbriggs was mostly built from the 19th century onwards and is a commuter town serving Glasgow. The name derives from land given to the Bishop of Glasgow, although there is argument about whether the second element refers to *briggs* (the Scots word for 'bridges') or *riggs* (the Scots word for 'fields'). Bishopbriggs is also home to the publishers HarperCollins, noted for their excellent dictionaries and books about Scotland.

Blair Atholl

Picturesque town in Perthshire, with the seat of
the Duke of Atholl, Blair Castle, nearby. The name
means 'the field of the new Ireland' with *blair* in
Gaelic meaning 'field' or 'plain' and *Atholl* historically
meaning 'New Ireland'.

Blairgowrie

Town in Perth and Kinross, known for growing
raspberries. The name 'Blairgowrie' means 'the plain
of Gowrie', but the origin of the place name 'Gowrie'
is unclear.

Black Isle

Peninsula in the Highlands, between the Moray Firth
and Beauly Firth to the south and the Cromarty Firth
to the north. Despite its name, the Black Isle is not an
island at all. The name is a translation of the Gaelic
An Eilean Dubh meaning 'the black island'. It has been
suggested that this is a reference to the fact that as a
peninsula it is surrounded on three sides by water and
that it has dark-coloured soil in comparison to the
neighbouring countryside.

Blantyre

Former mining town in Lanarkshire. Blantyre is famous for being the birthplace of African explorer and missionary David Livingstone. There is a much larger Blantyre in Malawi, the largest city in that country, with a population of over 700,000, which was named in honour of Livingstone's birthplace in 1891.

The name 'Blantyre' is of Brythonic origin and is believed to derive from *blaen tir* meaning 'edge of the land', in recognition to the area's proximity to the River Clyde.

Bonnybridge

Small town near Falkirk. Bonnybridge is famous for having more UFO sightings than anywhere else in Scotland. The name does not, sadly, derive from the town being 'bonny' in the Scots sense, or even an extra-terrestrial sense, but from the Gaelic *buan* meaning 'swift', a word that refers to the Bonny Water that was crossed by a bridge here.

Bo'ness

Former major port and town in West Lothian on the Firth of Forth, near the eastern end of the Antonine Wall. 'Bo'ness' is a contraction of the town's former and considerably less catchy name of Borrowstounness. That name derived from an Old English first name *Beornweard,* the Old English *tun* meaning 'farm', and the Old English *naes* meaning 'headland'.

Bowmore

Largest village on the island of Islay. Bowmore is best known as being the home for the Bowmore single malt whisky distillery, founded in 1779. The origin of the name is uncertain but is possibly from the Gaelic *botha more* meaning 'big house'.

Braemar

Town in Aberdeenshire on the River Dee that has become a popular tourist destination. Braemar is famous for the Braemar Gathering, the Highland Games held since 1832 and traditionally attended by the Royal Family. It was at Braemar that the Jacobite standard was raised for the unsuccessful 1715 uprising. The name derives from the Gaelic *braigh* meaning 'uplands', although the meaning of *Mar,* which is also the root of the Scottish surname Marr, is unknown.

Brechin

Historic town in Angus. Brechin is famous for its 14th-century cathedral that incorporates an even earlier round tower. Famous people born in Brechin include radar pioneer Robert Watson-Watt.

The origin of 'Brechin' is unclear, but it is possibly a Pictish or Brythonic name derived from a person called Brychan or Brachan.

Broughty Ferry

Seaside suburb of Dundee that was a separate town until 1913. The name 'Broughty' derives from the Gaelic *bruach* meaning 'bank' and *Tatha* being the Gaelic name of the River Tay. The English word 'Ferry' was added later, and reflects the fact that Broughty Ferry was the northern ferry port for crossing the Firth of Tay in the days before the Tay Bridge.

Buccleuch

Area in the Borders that gives its name to a dukedom. The title of Duke of Buccleuch was created in 1643 and is held by the Scott family. Buccleuch is pronounced 'buck-lew' (with the stress on the second syllable) and derives from the Scots *buck cleugh* which means 'deer ravine'.

Buchan

Historic area of Aberdeenshire that has been an earldom since at least the 12th century. Buchan is known for being a heartland of the distinctive Doric dialect and of the fishing and farming industries. Appropriately, it is thought that Buchan might derive from the Brythonic *buwch* meaning 'place of the cow' or from the Gaelic word *baoghan* meaning 'calf'.

Buchan has also become a common surname and is particularly associated with John Buchan, the Scottish author of *The Thirty Nine Steps*.

Buckie

Town on the Moray Firth and formerly a major fishing port. The name 'Buckie' is thought to derive from either *bocaidh*, the Gaelic word for 'whelk', or *buckie*, the Scots word for 'whelk'. The Fife fishing town of Buckhaven could have the same gastropodous origins.

Bute

Island in the Firth of Clyde. Bute was formerly a county in its own right, but is now part of Argyll and Bute. The island is a popular tourist destination and gave its name to the titles of Earl and (later) Marquess of Bute. John Stuart, the 3rd Earl of Bute, was briefly

British Prime Minister in 1762, the first Scot ever to hold that position, and the Stuarts of Bute would build the grand country house Mountstuart on the island as their family seat.

The name 'Bute' is thought to derive from the Norse *bot* meaning simply 'piece of land'.

Cairngorms

Mountain range in the Highlands. The Cairngorms are part of the Cairngorms National Park, opened in 2003, that is the largest national park in the United Kingdom. The mountains take their name from one specific peak, the Cairn Gorm, which means 'the blue hill', and therefore the name 'Cairngorms' in English means 'the blue hills'. Somewhat confusingly, the Gaelic name for the mountain range is *Am Monadh Ruadh*, which is translated as 'the red hills', and so perhaps we should declare that the Cairngorms have now become purple.

Caithness

Northeasternmost area of the Highlands and the Scottish mainland. Caithness has been an ancient earldom of first Norway and then Scotland since the 11th century, although the name derives from an earlier Pictish region called *Cat* that was either named after a Pictish leader or after the feline animal. The *ness* element of the name was added by the Vikings and means 'headland', therefore giving us 'headland of the cat'.

Callanish

Historic group of standing stones on the Isle of Lewis. The site contains a central group of 13 stones forming a circle around a burial cairn. The stone circle takes its name from the nearby village of Callanish (called *Calanais* in Gaelic). According to legend the stones are giants who were turned to stone for failing to convert to Christianity, and the Gaelic name for the stones is *Fir Bhreig* meaning 'false men'. The name 'Callanish' itself, however, is thought to derive from the Norse *Kalladarnes* meaning 'the ferry headland'.

Calder

Name of several place names in Scotland, including the three West Lothian towns of West Calder, Mid Calder and East Calder. There is also a River Calder in England and the name is believed to derive from the Brythonic *caled* meaning 'hard' and the Gaelic *dobhar* meaning 'water', although the Gaelic *call* meaning 'hazel wood' has also been suggested, and it is possible that different Calders around the country have different origins. Calder is also a common Scottish surname.

Callander

Town in Stirling. Callander is a popular tourist destination, rejoicing in the twin titles of 'The Gateway to the Trossachs' and 'The Gateway to the Highlands'. The name 'Callander' is of uncertain origin, but possibly shares the same derivation as Calder (explained in the previous entry). Callander became better known in the 1960s as the location for the fictional town of Tannochbrae, the setting for *Doctor Finlay's Casebook*.

Cambuslang

Former industrial town in South Lanarkshire, now a suburb of Glasgow. The name 'Cambuslang' derives from the Gaelic *camus* meaning 'bay' and *luinge* meaning 'ship'. The name refers to the fact that boats or ships could sail up the River Clyde to the original settlement.

Carluke

Historic town in South Lanarkshire that grew as an industrial area in the 19th century. The first part of the name derives from the Brythonic *caer* meaning 'fort', but it is unclear what *luke* means. It seems unlikely, however, that is has any connection with the biblical Saint Luke.

Carnoustie

Town in Angus that is the site of a famous golf course. Carnoustie has hosted the Open Golf Championship seven times and is sometimes nicknamed 'Carnasty' because of the perceived difficulty of the course.

The meaning of 'Carnoustie' is disputed: it may derive from the Gaelic *carn fheusta* meaning 'cairn of the feast' or else from *carn ghiutasiach* meaning 'cairn of the pine trees'.

Carrick

Area in South Ayrshire. Carrick was a historic earldom, held by the Bruce family before Robert the Bruce gained the Scottish crown. The title of Earl of Carrick is still retained by the Royal Family, with Prince Charles being the current earl. 'Carrick' derives from the Gaelic name *Carraig* meaning 'craggy place'. (The same origin can also be found in opening part of the Northern Irish town of Carrickfergus.)

Carron

Name of several places in Scotland, the most famous being Loch Carron in the Highlands and the River Carron in Central Scotland.

The Highland Loch Carron is a sea loch in Wester Ross fed by another River Carron. Settlements on the loch include Lochcarron, Strathcarron, Plockton, and the wonderfully named Stromeferry (which in Gaelic means 'no ferry', as there is no ferry from the settlement).

The Lowland River Carron gives its name to the famous Carron Ironworks near Falkirk, founded in 1769 and at the start of the 19th century the largest ironworks in Britain.

The name 'Carron' is of ancient origin and is thought to mean 'rough water'.

Castle Douglas

Town in Dumfries and Galloway. Castle Douglas was developed by merchant William Douglas in the 18th century. In fact, there is no castle in the town, but the ruined 14th-century Douglas stronghold of Threave Castle is only two miles away.

Cathcart

Suburb of Glasgow to the south of the River Clyde, formerly a village in its own right. The name 'Cathcart' derives from either the Brythonic *coet* meaning 'wood' or *caer* meaning 'fort', with *Cart* coming from the name of the river on which the original settlement was built.

Cawdor

Highland village near Nairn. Cawdor is famous for the title of 'Thane of Cawdor', which was one of the titles that Shakespeare gave Macbeth in his Scottish play. In fact, the title of 'Thane of Cawdor' did not exist until several centuries after the real-life Macbeth, and the historic Cawdor Castle was only built from the 14th century onwards, becoming a stronghold of the Clan Campbell. The name 'Cawdor' is actually a variation on the place name 'Calder', which is found throughout Scotland, and is believed to derive from the Brythonic *caled* meaning 'hard' and the Gaelic *dobhar* meaning 'water'.

Clackmannan

Small town in central Scotland that gives its name to the local-government region of Clackmannanshire. The name comes from the Gaelic *clach manna* meaning 'stone of Manau', with the meaning of 'Manau' being unknown, although it is probably a person's name.

Clyde

River in the west of Scotland. The River Clyde is the third longest river in Scotland, rising in Lanarkshire and flowing through Glasgow into the Firth of

Clyde. The river was deepened in the 18th century to take into account the rise of Glasgow as a major international trading port and to allow the entry of larger ships.

The origin of the name 'Clyde' is possibly Brythonic, meaning 'cleansing'. The river is called *Clutha* in Gaelic, as in the famous Glasgow pub The Clutha Vaults.

Clyde can be used as a male first name. Famous Clydes include West Indian cricketer Clyde Walcott, American outlaw Clyde Barrow, and Clint Eastwood's orang-utan in the film *Every Which Way But Loose*.

The fertile valley of the Clyde is called Clydesdale, and gives its name both to a large working horse that was used for ploughing and to the Clydesdale Bank, founded in 1838 and still producing its own banknotes.

The area around the Clyde is often known as called Clydeside. Clydeside became synonymous with the steel and shipbuilding industries in the 19th and the first half of the 20th century. 'Red Clydeside' was a term referring to the political radicalism around the Clyde shipyards during and immediately after the First World War.

Clydebank

Industrial town on the north bank of the River Clyde. The town was almost completely destroyed by the Luftwaffe in 1941 during the Second World War. Clydebank is also where the group Wet Wet Wet hail from, and is apparently a romantic place as 'Love Is All Around'.

Coatbridge

Town in North Lanarkshire. Coatbridge grew in the 19th century through the coal, iron, and steel industries. The name means literally 'bridge built next to cottages', as *cotts* is an old English word for 'cottages'.

Coldstream

Town on the River Tweed. Coldstream has long been a border crossing point to England and is best known for the Coldstream Guards, a regiment of the Household Division of the British Army, which has been in active service since its founding in 1650. The regiment was founded in Coldstream as part of the English Parliament's 'New Model Army' at the time of the English Civil War, and in 1658 moved from Coldstream to London to help bring about the restoration of the Stuart monarchy. As part of their duties the Coldstream Guards guard the royal properties in London, such as Windsor Castle and Buckingham Palace.

The name 'Coldstream' is, as you might imagine, a reference to the temperature of the River Tweed.

Coll

Hebridean island lying to the west of Mull. The name 'Coll' is of uncertain origin. One suggestion is that it derives from the Gaelic *colla* meaning 'high'; another is that it comes from the Norse *kollr* meaning 'summit' (although the island is not especially hilly).

Colonsay

Island in the Inner Hebrides, ancestral home of the Clan MacFie. It is believed that the island is named after Saint Columba, the 6th-century Irish missionary, with the ending 'ay' deriving from the Norse *ey* meaning 'island'.

Cowal

Peninsula in Argyll between Loch Fyne and Loch Long. The name 'Cowal' is believed to derive from the Irish first name *Comhgal*, meaning 'joint pledge'. Comhgal is said to have been a grandson of Fergus, the first King of Dalriada. Happily for the residents,

X Factor judge Simon Cowell is thought to have no connection with the peninsula.

Cowdenbeath

Town in Fife, formerly known for mining. The name possibly derives from a person called Cowden, combined with the Gaelic word *beith* meaning 'birches'.

Crail

Tourist and former fishing village in the East Neuk of Fife. The name 'Crail' is of uncertain origin as it dates back to Pictish times. Possible explanations are that it derives from the Gaelic *carr* meaning 'rock', or else from the older Brythonic *caer* meaning 'fort'.

Crianlarich

Town and tourist destination in Stirling, near Loch Lomond. Crianlarich is best known for being a popular stopping-off point for tourists en route to the North and West Highlands. The name 'Crianlarich' derives from the Gaelic *crion* meaning 'little' and *lairig* meaning 'pass'.

Crieff

Market town in Perth and Kinross that used to
hold one of the largest cattle markets in Scotland.
The name 'Crieff' means 'place among the trees',
deriving from the Gaelic *craoibh* meaning 'trees'.
Famous people born in Crieff include film star Ewan
McGregor and his actor uncle Denis Lawson who
starred in the film *Local Hero*.

Cromarty

Coastal village and former fishing port in the Black
Isle, and part of the former county of Ross and
Cromarty. The name 'Cromarty' derives from the
Gaelic *crom* meaning 'crooked' and *baigh* meaning
'bay', thereby giving us 'crooked bay'. Another
Gaelic word *aird*, meaning 'height', was added later,
so making Cromarty 'the crooked bay between the
heights'.

The Cromarty Firth is a sea inlet with Cromarty on its
south bank. The sheltered waters have been utilized in
the two World Wars as a naval base. Since the 1970s,
however, they have proved a boon to the oil industry,
with an oil depot at Nigg and an oil-rig repair yard at
Invergordon.

Cuillins

Mountain range on the Isle of Skye. The Cuillins form
one of the most famous and formidable mountain
ranges in Scotland, including twelve Munros, making
them a popular destination for walkers and climbers.
There are actually two ranges in the Cuillins, with
the Black Cuillins being the main and higher group,
and the Red Cuillins standing to the east. The name
'Cuillin' is believed to derive from the Irish hero
Cuchulainn, who trained as a warrior on the Isle of
Skye. Another possible explanation of the name is that
it might derive from the Norse word *kiolen* meaning
'high rocks'.

Culloden

Small village three miles east of Inverness. The village
of Culloden itself would be unremarkable had it not
given its name to a boggy moor three miles to the
south that was the site of the last battle, to date, to
have taken place on the British mainland. On 17th
April 1746 the remnants of Charles Edwards Stewart's
Jacobite army were annihilated here by the British
army, with a large percentage of Lowland Scots in
their ranks, led by the Duke of Cumberland, later
known as 'The Butcher', who instructed his men to
take no Jacobite prisoners. The battlefield of Culloden
Moor is now part of a National Trust visitor centre

and is a popular tourist attraction.

The name 'Culloden' derives from the Gaelic *cul* meaning 'back' and *lodair* meaning 'little pool'.

Culross

Historic town in Fife, on the Firth of Forth. Culross is actually pronounced 'coo-ros' with the 'l' being silent. The town was formerly an important trading port and is the possible birthplace of the patron saint of Glasgow, Saint Kentigern, who was better known as Saint Mungo. The name 'Culross' possibly means 'holly wood', deriving from the Gaelic *culeann* meaning 'holly' and the Brythonic *ros* meaning 'wood' (although the second part of the name could also perhaps be derived from the Gaelic *ros* meaning 'point').

Cults

Village and suburb of the city of Aberdeen. Sadly, the name 'Cults' does not derive from any groups with unusual religious beliefs, but comes either from the Gaelic *cuil* meaning 'corner' or the Brythonic *coit* meaning 'wood' (although who is to say what may or may not have taken place in the woods many centuries ago?). The Scottish surname Coutts derives from this place name.

Culzean

Castle and country park in Ayrshire. Culzean Castle was designed by Robert Adam in the 18th century and is one of the most famous and often-visited castles in Scotland. The name 'Culzean' is pronounced 'cull-ane', with the 'z' being silent, and derives from the original 14th-century tower house that was called *Cullean*, meaning 'place of caves', in reference to the nearby caves in the area.

Cumbernauld

New town in North Lanarkshire, established in 1956 to accommodate the relocation of people from Glasgow. Cumbernauld was previously a village with the name coming from the Gaelic *commain nan allt* meaning 'where the streams meet' as it is situated between streams that flow into both the Clyde and the Forth. Cumbernauld is known for its self-promotional catchphrase 'What's it called? Cumbernauld!' and was also the setting for the 1981 film *Gregory's Girl*, which depicted a teenage boy's infatuation with a girl who played in his school football team. The football team Clyde plays at Cumbernauld, but Dee Hepburn will not be found among its players.

Cumnock

Town in Ayrshire. Cumnock was formerly an important mining area. The name possibly derives from the Gaelic *cam cnoc* meaning 'crooked hill'.

Cunninghame

District of Ayrshire. The name may be derived from the Gaelic word *cuinneag* meaning 'milk-pail'. The surname Cunningham takes its name from the district.

Cupar

Historic town and former county town of Fife. The name 'Cupar' is of uncertain origin, although it has been suggested that it derives from the Gaelic *comhpairt* meaning 'common grazing land'.

The smaller town of Coupar Angus is so named to differentiate it from the Fife town of Cupar, although confusingly Coupar Angus is not actually in Angus, but in Perth and Kinross.

Currie

Suburb of Edinburgh. Until recently Currie was a village in its own right and has the Heriot-Watt University campus nearby. The place derives its name either from the Brythonic *curi* meaning 'hollow' or the Gaelic *curagh* meaning 'wet plain'. Famous people with the surname Currie include former Conservative politician Edwina Currie.

Dalkeith

Administrative centre of Midlothian. Dalkeith takes its name from the Brythonic *dol coed* meaning 'field by the wood'. Dalkeith Palace was the residence of the Dukes of Buccleuch. Famous people born in Dalkeith include 18th-century politician Henry Dundas, known as the 'uncrowned king of Scotland', and Fish, lead singer of the rock group Marillion.

Dallas

Village in Moray. This tiny village of around 150 people is somewhat overshadowed by the eponymous Texan city of 1.2 million, founded in 1856. The Scottish village gave its name to the surname Dallas, and the American city was named after the American Vice-President George Miffin Dallas, whose family originally came from the north-east of Scotland.

In recent times Dallas became infamous as the scene of the 1963 assassination of President John Kennedy, and then even better known for the popular television series *Dallas* which chronicled the lives and loves of a

Texan oil dynasty led by the very Scottish-sounding Jock Ewing.

The name 'Dallas' derives from the Gaelic *dail eas* meaning 'place by the waterfall'.

Dee

River that rises in the Cairngorms and flows into the North Sea at Aberdeen. The Dee is the fifth longest river in Scotland and is popular for salmon fishing. The area around the Dee is known as Royal Deeside due to its connections with the estates of Braemar and Ballater and the royal family's annual summer residence at Balmoral.

The origin of the name 'Dee' is unclear and probably Brythonic. There are several other rivers in Britain with the same name, and it has been suggested that the name might have meant 'goddess'.

Dingwall

Highland town, formerly the county town of Ross and Cromarty. Dingwall derives its name from the Norse *thing vollr*, with *thing* meaning 'assembly' or 'parliament' and *vollr* meaning 'field'. A similar Norse name *Tynwald* is the name of the parliament of the Isle of Man. Famous people born in Dingwall include the Scottish king Macbeth.

Don

River that lies north of the River Dee, rising in the Grampians and flowing into the North Sea at the Bridge of Don in the north of Aberdeen. There is also a River Don in Yorkshire, and both rivers are believed to share the same meaning of 'goddess'. 'The Dons' is also the nickname of Aberdeen Football Club, but it now some years since they have played in a divine manner.

Dornoch

Historic town on the north-east coast, formerly the county town of Sutherland. Dornoch Cathedral dates from the 13th century and was the location of the christening of Madonna's son Rocco on the day before her wedding in nearby Skibo Castle in 2000.

Dornoch Firth is the name of a sea inlet that separates Sutherland from Ross and Cromarty with Dornoch on its north shore.

The name 'Dornoch' derives from the Gaelic *dornach* meaning 'pebbles' – although today the beaches are mostly sandy.

Drumnadrochit

Village on the western shore of Loch Ness. Drumnadrochit is a popular tourist destination with both Urquhart Castle and a certain reclusive monster nearby. The name 'Drumnadrochit' derives from the Gaelic and means 'ridge by the bridge', with *druim* meaning 'ridge', *na* meaning 'by the', and *drochaid* meaning 'bridge', in reference to a bridge across the River Enrick.

Dryburgh

Name of a village in the Borders and an area of Dundee. The Dryburgh in the Borders is famous for the ruined 12th-century Dryburgh Abbey, which is (along with Melrose, Jedburgh, and Kelso) one of the four famous abbeys of the Scottish Borders, and the site of the burial plot of Sir Walter Scott. The Dundonian Dryburgh is famous for being the home of the rock band The View.

The name 'Dryburgh' is believed to derive from the Old English *dryge* meaning 'fort' and *burgh* meaning 'town'.

Dufftown

Town in Moray. Dufftown is one of the main centres of the malt-whisky industry, and is home to several distilleries. The town was named after James Duff, the fifth Earl of Fife, who founded it in 1817. Duff was a member of the Clan MacDuff, who long held the title of Thane of Fife (and feature as such in William Shakespeare's *Macbeth*). The surname 'Duff' derives from the Gaelic *duibh* meaning 'black'.

Dumbarton

Historic town on the north bank of the Clyde. Dumbarton was the capital of Strathclyde, an ancient kingdom of the Britons, from the 5th century until it was added to Scotland in the 11th century. The kingdom was ruled from a royal castle and fortress that sat on top of Dumbarton Rock. Dumbarton would later become a major shipbuilding town and its famous sons include Jackie Stewart, the former world motor-racing champion, and David Byrne, the lead singer of Talking Heads.

Dumbarton should technically be called 'Dunbarton' as the name comes from the Gaelic *dun breatainn* meaning 'fort of the Britons'. The Britons themselves called their capital 'Alcluith' meaning 'rock of the Clyde'.

The region around Dumbarton is actually called 'Dunbartonshire' rather than 'Dumbartonshire' and is divided into two local-government regions: East Dunbartonshire and West Dunbartonshire.

Dumfries

Historic town in the south of Scotland. Dumfries Kirk was where Robert the Bruce killed John Comyn, his main rival to the vacant Scottish throne, in 1306 and was where Robert Burns was buried after his death in 1796. Dumfries is also the place where the inventor Kirkpatrick Macmillan is believed to have ridden the first ever bicycle in 1839. The name is believed to mean 'ridge of the thicket' (if one takes *dum* as deriving from the Gaelic *drum* meaning 'ridge'). However, if *dum* derives from the Gaelic *dun*, then 'Dumfries' is more likely to mean 'fortified woodland'.

Dumfries has the nickname of 'The Queen of the South', which is also the name of the local football club. People from Dumfries are called 'Doonhamers', from a Scots expression for 'down south', since its location at the southern end of Scotland means that there is nowhere further down for you to go.

Famous people born in Dumfries include the broadcaster Kirsty Wark.

Dunbar

Historic town in East Lothian. Now a popular commuter town serving Edinburgh, Dunbar derives its name from the Brythonic *din* meaning 'fort' and *barr* meaning 'height' or 'summit'. Dunbar was the location of a battle in 1650 when Oliver Cromwell's English army, despite being heavily outnumbered, defeated the Scots and proceeded to occupy the entire country.

Famous people born in Dunbar include pioneering conservationist John Muir. Dunbar is said to have more sunshine than any other place in Scotland and has therefore gained the nickname of 'Sunny Dunny'.

Dunblane

Picturesque town in Stirling, site of a 13th-century cathedral. The name 'Dunblane' means 'fort of Saint Blane' after the 6th-century Irish Saint Blane. Famous people born in the town include tennis players Andy and Jamie Murray.

Dundee

City in eastern Scotland, the country's fourth-largest city, and a burgh since 1191. Dundee possibly took its name from the Gaelic word *dun* meaning 'hill' or 'hill-fort' and the Gaelic word *deagh* meaning 'fire', perhaps in recognition of the beacons that were lit on Dundee's highest point, the Dundee Law. Other possible translations of the city's name include 'dark hill'.

Dundee was once known as the city of the three

J's – jam, jute, and journalism – that were its major industries at the end of the 19th century. It now rejoices in the title of 'City of Discovery' after Captain Scott's ship *The Discovery*, which was built in the city in 1901. *The Discovery* was used for Scott's Antarctic expedition of 1901 to 1904, from which it was able to return home safely, despite being stuck in ice for two years. The ship now resides as a tourist attraction at Discovery Point in the city.

People from Dundee are called Dundonians. Dundonians have their own dialect, and a pie that is not all that moist would be called 'eh dreh peh' in the local vernacular. Famous people born in Dundee include film actor Brian Cox.

The city is also known for Dundee cake, a rich fruit cake that is believed to originate there. Another culinary connection comes from the invention of marmalade there by the firm of Keillor's – the story goes that they received a double delivery of oranges and decided to make the best of it.

Arguably Britain's most famous Prime Minister, Winston Churchill, was elected Member of Parliament for Dundee in 1908. However it is fair to say that it was an uneasy relationship. Churchill lost his seat in the general election of 1922, when the Dundee electorate voted him into fourth place.

Dundee has two major football teams – Dundee

and Dundee United – who uniquely have their own football stadiums only 160 metres from each other. Dundee is also home to two universities – Dundee and Abertay – and the publishing firm of D.C. Thomson, which has given the world *The Beano, The Dandy* and *The Sunday Post* and with them such comic favourites as Dennis The Menace, Desperate Dan, Oor Wullie, and The Broons.

The phrase 'Bonnie Dundee' is sometimes applied to the city, but is most often associated with John Graham, the 1st Viscount Dundee, who led the first Jacobite rising in 1689 but was killed at the battle of Killiecrankie. Mick Dundee was the character played by Australian actor Paul Hogan in the 1986 film comedy *Crocodile Dundee*. Another famous holder of the name was Angelo Dundee, the great boxing trainer, who is known especially for his association with Muhammad Ali.

Dunfermline

Historic town in Fife and ancient capital of Scotland. Dunfermline is one of Scotland's earliest royal burghs and a royal residence from the 11th to the 17th century. Famous people born in Dunfermline include Charles I, king of England and Scotland from 1625 until his execution in 1649, Andrew Carnegie, who made his name in America as a steel magnate and philanthropist, and who gave his name to the Carnegie Hall, and singer and actress Barbara Dickson, who had an international hit with 'I Know Him So Well'.

Dunfermline takes its name from the Gaelic *dun fearam linn* that means 'the fort in the bend of the stream'.

Dunkeld

Historic town in Perth and Kinross. The relics of Saint Columba were brought to Dunkeld in the 9th century, and Dunkeld Cathedral was built over the site of his burial in the 12th century. Dunkeld was an important royal and religious centre in medieval Scotland and gave its name to the royal House of Dunkeld that held the monarchy from 1034, when Duncan I became the first king of a unified Scotland, to the death of Margaret the Maid in 1290.

The name 'Dunkeld' derives from the Gaelic and Pictish *dun* meaning 'fort' and the Gaelic *chailleainn* meaning 'of the Caledonions'.

Dunnottar

Dramatic ruined castle and fortress on the north-east coast of Scotland. Dunnottar Castle stands on a promontory two miles from Stonehaven and is one of the most famous castles in Scotland. A fortress had existed on the site since the 7th century and the building of the castle began in the 13th century by the Keith family, the Earls of Marischal. In 1651 the Honours of Scotland were brought to Dunnottar Castle for safe-keeping and then smuggled out when the castle was besieged by Cromwell's men. The 1990 film version of *Hamlet*, starring Mel Gibson, was filmed there.

The name 'Dunnottar' derives from the Pictish name *Dun Fother*, with *dun* meaning 'fort' and *fother* possibly meaning 'of the low country'.

Dunoon

Town and holiday resort in Argyll on the west bank of the Firth of Clyde. The town of Dunoon is next to Holy Loch, which was a controversial, if locally lucrative, American navy base from 1961 to 1992. The name 'Dunoon' derives from the Gaelic *dun* meaning 'fort' and *obhainn* meaning 'river'.

Duns

Town in the Borders and former county town of Berwickshire. The proud motto of the town is 'Duns dings a'' meaning 'Duns beats all', and people from Duns are called 'Dingers'. The name 'Duns' derives from the Gaelic *dun* meaning 'fort on the hill', and the original settlement of Duns was built on top of the hill called Duns Law.

Famous people born in Duns include acclaimed 13th-century theologian and philosopher John Duns Scotus. Over time, however, his views fell out of fashion and his supporters, who were called Dunses after the town of his birthplace, began to be criticized. Hence the origin of the term 'dunce' being used as a derogatory term for those considered incapable of becoming good scholars. It is not surprising, therefore, that the educated and wise people of Duns were so keen on having an alternative nickname – even if it happened to be 'Dingers'.

Durness

Highland village on the north coast of Sutherland. Durness was where John Lennon spent many of his childhood holidays and the name derives from the Norse *dyr* meaning 'deer' and *nes* meaning 'headland'.

East Kilbride

New town south of Glasgow. East Kilbride was a village until 1947 when development began on turning it into Scotland's largest town – only the cities of Glasgow, Edinburgh, Aberdeen, and Dundee having a larger population.

The name 'Kilbride' comes from the Gaelic meaning 'the church of Saint Bride'. Saint Bride or Saint Bridget was a 5th-century Irish nun known for her holiness and founding several convents in Ireland. Bride was also the name of a Celtic goddess of fire, and the preservation of the pagan name reflects the fact that the early Celtic church retained many of the pre-Christian religious traditions.

East Kilbride was so named to differentiate it from the village of West Kilbride that is found in Ayrshire. Famous people born in East Kilbride include television presenters Lorraine Kelly and Kirsty Young, who have both presented *Have I Got News for You*.

East Neuk

Area on the coast of south-east Fife. The 'East Neuk' is the name given to the group of small fishing villages that have become a popular tourist destination. Villages on the East Neuk include Crail, Anstruther, Pittenweem, St Monans, and Elie. The name derives from the Scots word for 'nook' or 'corner' in recognition of its location away from the major Fife towns (and no, before you ask, there is no North, South, or West Neuk).

Edinburgh

The capital of Scotland since the 15th century. Edinburgh is Scotland's second-largest city and is home to the Scottish Parliament and Government. The oldest surviving building in Edinburgh is Saint Margaret's Chapel at Edinburgh Castle, built in the 12th century, although there has been a military fortress at the Castle for more than a thousand years. Edinburgh University was founded in 1582 and there are now three other universities in the city: Heriot-Watt, Napier, and Queen Margaret.

The world renowned Edinburgh International Festival began in 1947, and was soon supplemented by the Edinburgh Festival Fringe, which began in the following year, and later by a book festival, film festival and numerous other festivals. The most popular event at the Festival remains the Edinburgh Military Tattoo that takes place at the Esplanade of the Edinburgh Castle.

Edinburgh used to be a Northumbrian town and was ruled by the Angles until captured by the Scots in 1018. Edinburgh's Gaelic name is *Dun Eideann*. *Dun* means 'hill fort', but what *Edin* meant in its original Northumbrian is unclear, although it might mean 'rock face' or be the personal name of a king or ruler. It has been suggested that *Edin* might refer to a Northumbrian king called Edwin, but the name of

Dun Edin predates the 7th century, when Edwin lived, so this is thought unlikely. *Burgh* is an English word meaning 'stronghold' or 'town' and the English word *Edinburgh* was used rather the Gaelic *Dun Eideann*. The Gaelic name was, however, taken up as the name of the city of Dunedin in New Zealand's South Island, and that city also shares many of Edinburgh's famous street names.

Edinburgh gained the nickname 'Auld Reekie' after the amount of smoke that would fill the sky on the occasions when the residents lit their coal fires and was also called 'The Athens of the North' in recognition of its dramatic historic landscape and the failed attempts to replicate a Greek style Acropolis on Calton Hill.

Famous people born in Edinburgh included James VI of Scotland, who became James I of England in 1603, renowned philosopher David Hume, renowned scientist James Clerk Maxwell, inventor of the telephone Alexander Graham Bell, leader of Dublin's 1916 Easter Rising James Connolly, birth-control pioneer Marie Stopes, film legend Sean Connery (who liked his Edinburgh accent so much that he kept it no matter what nationality of character he was playing), British Prime Minister Tony Blair, and 19th-century Skye terrier Greyfriars' Bobby (who may not have been born in Edinburgh, but whose gravestone and statue are amongst the most visited places in the city).

Edinburgh is also known for being the birthplace of famous authors Sir Walter Scott, Robert Louis Stevenson, Muriel Spark, and Irvine Welsh, and is the home of bestselling writers J.K. Rowling, Ian Rankin, and Alexander McCall Smith.

The first Scottish Parliament was built on the city's Royal Mile in 1640, but closed in 1707 after the Act of Union between the English and Scottish parliaments and was turned into the home of the Scottish judiciary. The second Scottish Parliament was opened in 2004 next to Holyrood Palace, which was built in the 16th century. The new Scottish Parliament was unfortunately not built at 16th-century prices.

Edinburgh is more strongly subject to English influence than other parts of Scotland, and residents are sometimes characterized as being reserved and over-refined – hence the famous saying about 'sex' being what posh Edinburgh people used to put their coal in.

A completely different side of Edinburgh was portrayed by author Irvine Welsh in the novel *Trainspotting*. This had plenty of sex, but could certainly not be characterized as being either reserved or refined.

The title of Duke of Edinburgh was first created in 1726, but has only been used sporadically by the British monarchy. None of the holders of the title have had any prior connection with either the city, or indeed with any part of Scotland. The current Duke (who has held the title since 1947) is the Queen's consort Prince Philip, who was born in Corfu.

Eigg

Island in the Inner Hebrides south of Skye. In 1997 the 80 or so residents of Eigg successfully completed a community buy-out of the island. The name 'Eigg' does not have any connection with eggs but possibly derives from the Gaelic *eag* meaning 'notch' or 'rift' in reference to the ridge that runs down the island from its highest point.

Eildons

Trio of hills in the Borders that overlook the town of Melrose. The Eildons contain remains of ancient forts and according to local legend is where King Arthur and the Knights of the Round Table lie sleeping. It is unclear where the name 'Eildon' comes from. *Don* is the Old English for 'hill', but there is no agreement on the first part, although it has been suggested (in line with the Eildons' mystical history) that *eil* might mean 'elves'.

Eilean Donan

Small islet on Loch Duich in the western Highlands. Eilean Donan is famous for being the location of one of the most photogenic of all Scottish castles. Eilean Donan Castle dates back to the 13th century and was owned first by the Clan MacKenzie then by the Clan MacRae. It has featured as the backdrop in numerous films, television series, and postcards. The name 'Eilean Donan' is Gaelic and means 'island of Donan', with Donan being the name of a 7th-century priest who brought Christianity to the western Highlands and the Hebrides.

Elgin

Historic town and royal burgh that is the administrative centre of Moray. A much larger Elgin (with a population of 100,000) is to be found in the American state of Illinois. The name is also famously associated with the Elgin Marbles, a collection of marble sculptures and ancient antiquities from the Acropolis in Athens that was appropriated by Thomas Bruce, the 7th Earl of Elgin, in the early 19th century, and which the British Government has consistently refused to return to Greece.

Elgin probably takes its name from the Gaelic word *elg* meaning 'Ireland', which would make Elgin 'Little Ireland'.

Ellon

Commuter town north of Aberdeen. The name 'Ellon' derives from the Gaelic *eilean* meaning 'island', referring to the fact that the town was built on a ford of the River Ythan.

Eriskay

Small Hebridean island between South Uist and Barra. It was at Eriskay that Charles Edward Stewart first landed on Scottish soil in 1745 with thoughts of reclaiming the British crown, and in 1941 the *SS Politician* ran aground there with a cargo of whisky, so inspiring the Compton Mackenzie novel *Whisky Galore*. The name 'Eriskay' is Norse in origin and means 'Erik's island'.

Erskine

Commuter town in Renfrewshire. The town is best known for the Erskine Bridge, built in 1971, that connects Dunbartonshire on the north bank of the Clyde to Renfrewshire on the south bank. The name 'Erskine' possibly derives from the Gaelic *ard sescenn* and means 'high marsh'.

Ettrick

River that rises in Dumfries and Galloway and flows into the River Tweed in the Borders. The river gives its name to the Borders district of Ettrick, the village of Ettrickbridge, and to Ettrick Forest, formerly one of Scotland's greatest forests and site of many a royal hunting expedition, but now sadly denuded of trees.

James Hogg, the author of *The Private Memoirs and Confessions of a Justified Sinner*, was born in Ettrick and was given the nickname 'The Ettrick Shepherd', referring to the occupation he pursued before he took up writing.

The name 'Ettrick' is of unclear origin, although it has been suggested that it might derive from the Brythonic *atre* meaning 'playful'.

Falkirk

Historic town in central Scotland. Two major battles took place at Falkirk: Bonnie Prince Charlie's Jacobites won a rare victory there in 1746, but in 1298 William Wallace's brief tenure as Guardian of Scotland came to an end there when the Scottish forces were defeated by the English forcing Wallace to go in to hiding.

Falkirk is today famous for the Falkirk Wheel, a rotating boatlift that opened in 2002, and for being one of the stops on the train line between Edinburgh and Glasgow. Fortunately, it is not compulsory to get off the train there.

The *kirk* in 'Falkirk' comes from the Scots word for 'church' and *fal* means 'field' or 'fold' so Falkirk is 'the field near the church'. The Gaelic name is *An Eaglais Bhreac*, which means 'the speckled church'.

Fife

Local-government authority between the Firth of Forth and the Firth of Tay. Fife was one of the earliest mormaerdoms or minor kingdoms of Scotland. The name is believed to derive from a man with Pictish name of *Fib*, who, according to legend, was one of the seven brothers who gave their names to the different regions of Pictland. People from Fife are called Fifers, and Fife is still today referred to as 'The Kingdom of Fife'.

Findhorn

Village on the Moray Firth. Findhorn is best known for being the home of The Findhorn Foundation, a community set up in 1962 and dedicated to a spiritual and ecological way of life. Findhorn lies where the River Findhorn joins Findhorn Bay, and the name derives from the Gaelic words *fionn* meaning 'white' and *eren* meaning 'water'.

Finnieston

Area of Glasgow on the north shore of the River Clyde. Finnieston gives its name to one of Glasgow's most famous landmarks – the Finnieston Crane. This cantilever crane was built in 1932 and stands over 160 feet high with a cantilever of over 250 feet long. The crane was originally built to lift very heavy parts for the shipbuilding industry, but has not been in use since the 1990s. The crane is actually sited on Stobcross Quay, but is known as the Finnieston Crane because of its proximity to Finnieston Quay. The name 'Finnieston' was given to the area in the 18th-century by the Orr family, who owned the land, in honour of their family tutor, John Finnie.

Fintry

The name of a picturesque village in Stirling between the Campsie Hills and the Fintry Hills, and also an area of Dundee. The name 'Fintry' derives from the Gaelic *fionn* meaning 'white' and the Brythonic *tref* meaning 'house'.

Forfar

Administrative centre of Angus. Forfar is famous for giving its name to the Forfar bridie, a meat pastry with optional onions, supposed to have been given its name

as it was cooked as a dish to be eaten at
wedding meals (which also explains the horseshoe
shape of the pastry). The name 'Forfar' itself possibly
derives from the Gaelic *faithir faire* meaning
'lookout hill'.

Forres

Historic town in Moray. According to William
Shakespeare's *Macbeth*, Forres was the location of
King Duncan's castle. The name 'Forres' is believed
to be identical with the name *Varris* recorded by the
Romans. However, the Gaelic name *Farrais* means
'beneath the bushes', a reference to the town's location
at the foot of forested hills.

Fort Augustus

Highland village at the south-west end of Loch Ness.
Fort Augustus is famous for a series of locks that
connects the Caledonian Canal to Loch Ness. The
village was formerly known as Kilchumin (or *Cill
Chuimein* in Gaelic), but was renamed in 1730 when
General Wade built a fort and barracks there after
the 1715 Jacobite rebellion. The Fort was not named
after the Roman Emperor Augustus, but after Prince
William Augustus, the second son of George II. This
man would later become infamous in Scotland as the
Duke of Cumberland, victor at the Battle of Culloden

in 1746, who earned the nickname of 'The Butcher' for his brutal treatment of the defeated Jacobites in the aftermath of the battle.

Forth

Major Scottish river that rises in the Trossachs and flows through Stirling into the Firth of Forth that separates Fife from Edinburgh. The famous Forth Bridge was opened in 1890 to carry rail traffic, with the Forth Road Bridge following in 1964. The Forth and Clyde Canal was opened in the 18th century and was Scotland's busiest canal, connecting Grangemouth in the east to the Firth of Clyde beyond Dumbarton in the west.

It is unclear whether the name 'Forth' has a Brythonic, Gaelic, or Norse origin, nor is it known what it means, or even whether the person who named it could count to more than four. The modern Gaelic name for the river is *Aibhainn Dhubh*, which means 'black river'.

Fort William

Town in the west Highlands. Fort William is a popular tourist destination due to its proximity to Ben Nevis and Glencoe and is the finishing line for walkers completing the West Highland Way. The town was built by Cromwell's troops in the 1650s at the time of the English occupation and was named 'Fort William' after King William III in the 1690s.

The town was then renamed first 'Gordonsburgh' and then 'Duncansburgh' before reverting to its original name after the Jacobite risings – this time in honour of Prince William, the Duke of Cumberland (the same man after whom Fort Augustus had been named). The Gaelic name for Fort William is *An Gearasdan*, which simply means 'The Garrison'.

Fraserburgh

Important fishing town on the north-east coast. Fraserburgh takes its name from the Fraser family, local landowners who built the town in the 16th century. Fraserburgh is known locally as 'The Broch', a Scots variation of 'burgh'.

Freuchie

Village in Fife. Freuchie is famous for producing Scotland's best-known cricket team, unlikely winner of the national village cricket championship at Lord's in 1985. The name 'Freuchie' derives from the Gaelic word *fraoch* meaning 'heather'.

Gairloch

Highland village on Loch Gairloch, a sea loch in Wester Ross, and popular tourist destination. The name derives from the Gaelic *gear* meaning 'short'.

The similarly named Gare Loch is a sea loch found further south, in Argyll. It has Helensburgh on its eastern shore, and is best known for being the home of the Faslane Naval Base, which once housed Polaris and now houses Trident nuclear submarines.

Galashiels

Town in the Borders. Known locally as simply 'Gala', Galashiels is noted for textile industries and rugby. The name derives from the Gala Water, on which the town is situated, and the Norse word *skalis* meaning 'shieldings' or 'sheds'. The name 'Gala' itself is believed to come from the Brythonic *gal gwy* meaning 'clear stream'.

The motto of Galashiels is 'soor plooms' and is said to refer to an incident in the 14th century when English raiders were defeated in a field of plum trees. The phrase was later applied to a sharp-flavoured sweet.

Galloway

Historic area in south-west Scotland. Galloway includes the former counties of Wigtownshire and

Kirkcudbrightshire and is now part of the Dumfries and Galloway local-government authority.

In the 5th century, Saint Ninian established a church in Whithorn in Galloway that is believed to be the first Christian church in Scotland. Galloway was to be an independent kingdom or sub-kingdom until the 13th century, being ruled by the Britons, the English, the Norse, and the MacFergus lords of Galloway. The Norse influence on Galloway between the 9th and 11th centuries is evident in the region's name which derives from the Gaelic *Gall-Gadal* and means 'land of the Gaelic-Norse'.

Famous Galloways include the Scottish politician 'Gorgeous' George Galloway and Galloway cattle, a Scottish breed of beef cattle. These latter are either all black or else black with a white band or belt around their middle, and are usually referred to as 'hardy' rather than 'gorgeous'.

Garry

Name of two rivers, one in Perthshire and one in the Highlands. The name is also found as a component of the names of associated glens and lochs. Invergarry is the name of a Highland village that means 'the mouth of the Garry' and was a stronghold for the Clan MacDonnell of Glengarry. The Glengarry bonnet or cap is usually dark blue with a red bobble, and has been .

favoured by Scottish regiments since the 19th century. *Glengarry Glen Ross* is also the name of a play by David Mamet about American estate agents. The name 'Garry' is of ancient origin and is thought to mean 'rough'.

Giffnock

Southern suburb of Glasgow and administrative centre of East Renfrewshire. The name 'Giffnock' derives from the Brythonic *cefn* meaning 'ridge' and *oc* meaning 'little'.

Girvan

Seaside and fishing town in Ayrshire. Girvan was once a popular holiday destination for Glaswegians in the days before cheap air travel to the Mediterranean. Boats from Girvan run to the nearby island of Ailsa Craig in the Firth of Clyde. There is no agreement on where the name 'Girvan' comes from, although it has been suggested that it may derive from the Brythonic word *gerw* meaning 'rough', although (as you might imagine) residents of Girvan are not especially keen on that translation.

Glamis

Historic village in Angus. The village is famous for Glamis Castle, owned by the Earls of Strathmore,

which was the childhood home of Queen Elizabeth, the Queen Mother, and the birthplace of Princess Margaret. Glamis also features in play *Macbeth*, where Shakespeare inaccurately claims that Macbeth was Thane of Glamis. Perhaps Shakespeare simply got his Scottish history mixed up as King Malcolm II (the king before Duncan, who was the king before Macbeth) was killed at Glamis in 1034. The name 'Glamis' derives from the Gaelic *glamhus* and means 'wide gap'. It is pronounced 'glams', with the 'i' being silent.

Glasgow

Port in the west of Scotland, the country's largest city. Glasgow was founded in the 6th century when Saint Kentigern (also known as Saint Mungo) established a church in the kingdom of Strathclyde, then inhabited by Britons. The name 'Glasgow' derives from the Brythonic name *Glascau* meaning 'green hollow' or alternatively 'dear green place'. The latter translation comes from the Gaelic name *Glaschu* and was the name of a classic novel by Archie Hind. To this day locals will call their city 'Glesca' or 'Glesga'.

Glasgow became a burgh in 1175. Its cathedral was built in the 13th century and Glasgow University was founded in 1451 (other universities in Glasgow are Strathclyde and Caledonian University). In the 19th century Glasgow became one of the most important industrial cities in the world, at the forefront of the steel and shipbuilding industries, and gave itself the title of 'Second City of the British Empire', hosting the Empire Exhibition of 1938. The popular song 'I Belong to Glasgow' was written by entertainer Will Fyffe.

A 'Glasgow kiss' can be both a romantic gesture and a less-than-romantic head-butt. This latter meaning suggests an affinity with violence that is also found in the phrase 'no mean city', which became commonly used after being the title of a classic 1935 novel by Alexander McArthur and H. Kingsley Long. In the 1980s the city made a concerted attempt to shake off this violent image with the 'Glasgow's Miles Better' campaign, and culminating in Glasgow becoming the European City of Culture in 1990. However, crime remains associated with Glasgow in the form of the television detective series *Taggart*, which has run since 1984 and is famous for the catchphrase 'There's been a murder'.

People from Glasgow are called Glaswegians. Famous Glaswegians include iconic artist, architect, and designer Charles Rennie Mackintosh, football manager Alex Ferguson, and comedian and actor Billy Connolly.

Connolly and his fellow Glaswegian comedians

Stanley Baxter and Rikki Fulton have made Glasgow famous as a city of humour, and the humorous aspect of the local dialect has been celebrated in books such as Baxter's *Parliamo Glasgow* and Michael Munro's *The Patter*. A typical Glaswegian joke involves a man on a high bridge meeting another who says he is feeling dizzy. The first man asks the dizzy man, 'Have you got vertigo?', to which the second replies, 'No, I live just round the corner.'

Port Glasgow is a town in Inverclyde that was developed from 1667 onwards as a deep-water port and shipbuilding centre for the growing city of Glasgow.

Glencoe

Mountainous valley and village in the Lochaber region. The valley of Glencoe is ten miles long and lies between Rannoch Moor and Loch Leven. Renowned for its dramatic beauty, it is a long-standing tourist destination and is popular with hill-walkers. Glencoe is also infamous for the massacre that took place there in February 1692, when 39 members of the Clan MacDonald were murdered by British troops to make an example of the clan for their tardiness in swearing allegiance to King William III. The troops accepted the hospitality of the MacDonalds, who were unaware of the true purpose of their presence in the Glen, for twelve days before attacking them in their beds.

The name 'Glencoe' is often said to mean 'the Glen of weeping' in reference to the massacre, but in fact the name either derives from the River Coe that runs through the valley or means 'narrow valley' from the Gaelic words *glean* meaning 'valley' and *comhann* meaning 'narrow'.

Glenfinnan

Village at the foot of Glen Finnan in Lochaber at the northern end of Loch Shiel. Glenfinnan is famous for being the place where Charles Edward Stewart raised the Jacobite standard on the 19th of August 1745. A monument was erected to commemorate the event in 1815. Glenfinnan is also famous for being a stop on the West Highland railway line. The 100-feet high Glenfinnan Viaduct that was completed in 1901 and featured as a backdrop in the *Harry Potter* films. Glenfinnan was also the fictional birthplace of the 'Immortal' Connor MacLeod from the *Highlander* films.

The name 'Glenfinnan' is often thought to derive from the personal name *Fingon*, a descendant of Kenneth MacAlpine, who is said to be the founder of the Clan MacKinnon.

Glenrothes

Administrative centre of Fife. Glenrothes was Scotland's second new town when it was founded in 1949. The name 'Glenrothes' derives from the Earls of Rothes, who were local landowners in Fife. The Earls of Rothes were Leslies who also owned land in north-east Scotland and took their name from the Moray town of Rothes, whose name means 'ringed fort' (from the Gaelic word *rath*). The *Glen* part of the name was added to differentiate the Fife Rothes from the Moray Rothes, even though there is no glen as such – although the town is in the Leven valley.

Glenrothes has proved successful in attracting electronic and new-technology industries to the area and is often associated with the phrase 'Silicon Glen', although this term applies more generally to the entire Central Belt of Scotland. Famous people born in Glenrothes include film actor Dougray Scott.

Golspie

Highland village in Sutherland on the shores of the Moray Firth. The name 'Golspie' is Norse in origin. It probably derives from a personal name *Goll* and means 'Goll's settlement' or 'Goll's town'.

Gorbals

Area of central Glasgow south of the River Clyde.
The Gorbals became known in the 19th and 20th
centuries as a densely populated working-class
tenement area that included large numbers of Catholic
Irish immigrants. Since the Second World War, there
have been several attempts at redevelopment, with
mixed results to date. *Growing Up in the Gorbals* is a
well-known autobiography by Ralph Glasser. Michael
Martin, the Speaker of the House of Commons, is
sometimes called 'Gorbals Mick' in a derogatory
reference to his working-class Glaswegian background,
although he has never lived in the area.

The area takes its name from the Gaelic name *Gort a
Bhaile* meaning 'field of the town'.

Gordon

District of Aberdeenshire. Gordon takes its name from
the Gordon family who originated in Berwickshire
and became landowners in the north-east of Scotland
from the 13th century onwards, gaining the title
of Earl of Huntly in the 15th century. The original
Gordons took their name from a place in Berwickshire
which either came from the Gaelic *gor dun* or the
Brythonic *gor din* both of which mean 'hill fort'.

Gordon gave its name to the Gordon Highlanders,

one of Scotland's most famous regiments, first raised in 1794, and who acquired the nickname 'The Gay Gordons'. This in turn became the name of a lively Scottish dance popular at weddings.

Famous Gordons include comic-strip hero Flash Gordon, 'mad, bad and dangerous to know' poet George Gordon Byron (better known as Lord Byron), the unfortunate General Charles Gordon, who died at Khartoum in the Sudan, chef Gordon Ramsay, and Prime Minister (at least at the time of writing) Gordon Brown.

Govan

Area of Glasgow, famous for shipbuilding. Govan became part of Glasgow in 1912, and was previously a separate town of long-standing. The Gaelic name for Govan is *Baille a Ghobhainn*, which means 'smith's town', although other theories have Govan meaning 'a ditch' or 'excellent ale'. Perhaps a combination of the two might make the most sense. Ibrox Park, the home of Rangers Football Club, is found in Govan. In recent years Govan has become famous for the by-elections of both 1973 and 1988 when the Scottish National Party won this traditionally Labour seat, only to lose it again at the following general election.

Famous sons of Govan include comedian Billy Connolly and football manager Alex Ferguson.

Grampian

Area of north-east Scotland. Grampian was the name of a local-government authority that existed from 1975 to 1996 and included Aberdeen, Aberdeenshire and Moray. Grampian Television was the name of the ITV company that broadcast to the north-east of Scotland until 2006.

The region took its name from the Grampian Mountains and many have assumed that the mountains are to be found in the same area around Aberdeenshire. However, the Grampians make up a geographical area that occupies nearly half of the Scottish mainland and includes the central Highlands as well as north-east Scotland and incorporates both the Cairngorms and Scotland's two highest peaks, Ben Nevis in the west and Ben Macdui in the east.

The name 'Grampian' arises from a misinterpretation of the Roman name *Graupius*, first used by the historian Tacitus with reference to a major battle that took place around AD83 and resulted in victory for the Roman army led by Agricola over a Caledonian army led by a chieftain called Calgacus. Tacitus calls the site of the battle *Mons Graupius*, but its location is unknown, although is believed to be somewhere in Aberdeenshire.

Grangemouth

Industrial town on the River Forth in the Falkirk region. Grangemouth is home to one of the largest oil refineries in Europe and is also one of the busiest container ports in Britain, with most of Scotland's fuel stocks currently being supplied from there. The town was founded in 1769 to coincide with the construction of the Forth and Clyde Canal and takes its name from the Grange Burn that flows into the Forth, with the name referring to the grange of Newbattle Abbey.

Famous people born in Grangemouth include former *Loose Women* presenter Kaye Adams, although this was in no way a comment on the female population of the town.

Grantown-on-Spey

Highland town and holiday resort in Speyside. Grantown-on-Spey was founded on the River Spey by Ludovic Grant in 1765 and was named after the Grant family.

Greenock

Town on the Clyde and administrative centre of Inverclyde. Greenock either takes its name from the Gaelic *grianaig* meaning 'sunny bay' or *griancnoc*

meaning 'sunny hill'. Famous people born in Greenock include James Watt, whose work on the steam engine ushered in the Industrial Revolution, sea-captain-turned-pirate William Kidd, and actor Richard Wilson.

Laconic comedian Chic Murray was also born in Greenock. Once, when visiting London, Murray was asked by a stranger looking for directions, 'Do you know the Battersea Dogs' Home?' to which he replied, 'I didn't know he was away.'

Gretna

Village on the border with England. It is most famous for Gretna Green, where young eloping couples from England could take advantage of Scotland's more liberal laws concerning marriage – neither ministers nor permission from respective parents were required – and presumably would enjoy a honeymoon in Gretna immediately afterwards. Gretna has recently found additional fame through the spectacular rise and equally spectacular fall of its football club.

The name 'Gretna' is believed to come from the Old English name *Greten ho* which means 'place of the gravelly hill'.

Greyfriars

Historic kirk and graveyard in Edinburgh. Greyfriars has been made famous by the true story of the Skye Terrier called Greyfriars' Bobby, who faithfully guarded his master's grave for 14 years before on his own death being buried in the kirkyard.

Greyfriars Kirk was built in the early 1600s and in 1638 was the location for the signing of Scotland's National Covenant. Although Greyfriars was built after the Reformation, the name derives from a pre-Reformation friary of the Franciscan order. (The Franciscans were known as the Grey Friars after the colour of their habits.)

Haddington

Administrative centre of East Lothian. Haddington is a historic town and was one of Scotland's first royal burghs in the 12th century. Its name derives from a personal name *Hada* (of either Old English or Danish origin) and the Old English word *inga* meaning 'people', thus giving a possible meaning of 'town of Hada's people'. Famous people born in Haddington include Scotland's best-known Protestant reformer, John Knox.

Hamilton

Administrative centre of South Lanarkshire. Hamilton was previously known as Cadzow but changed its name in honour of James Hamilton, the 1st Lord Hamilton, who died in 1479. The Hamiltons would later become the Douglas-Hamiltons and were given the title of Duke of Hamilton in 1643. Unrelated famous Hamiltons include motor-racing driver Lewis Hamilton.

One of the most famous parliamentary by-elections in Scottish history took place at Hamilton in 1967 when Winnie Ewing won the seat for the Scottish National Party.

There are two larger Hamiltons in the world: Hamilton in Ontario, Canada, has a population of over 600,000, and the city of Hamilton in New Zealand's North Island has a population of over 100,000. Hamilton is also the name of the capital of Bermuda.

The surname Hamilton is not originally Scottish but came from the Anglo-French family of de Hameldon, who also had land in Hambledon in Hampshire. The name 'Hambledon' derives from the Old English *hamel dun* meaning 'crooked hill'.

Hampden Park

Football stadium in the south of Glasgow. Hampden Park has been the home ground of the Scottish national football team (as well as local Glasgow club, Queen's Park) since 1903. Until 1950, Hampden was the largest football stadium in the world, with its highest attendance being the massive 149,000 people who watched the match between Scotland and England in 1937. The stadium has become famous for 'the Hampden Roar', the volume of noise that the Scottish crowd can produce (even though the current stadium capacity is only 52,000).

There were two much smaller Hampden Parks before the 1903 stadium was built. The first Hampden Park was built in 1873 on land that had previously been called Hampden Terrace. Interestingly, for what would become such a Scottish institution, Hampden Terrace had been named after an English politician, John Hampden, who was a leader of the parliamentarians in the English Civil War. Hampden is the name of a place in the English county of Buckinghamshire, and means 'homestead valley'.

Harris

Southern part of Lewis and Harris in the Outer Hebrides. Contrary to commonly held belief, Harris is not a separate island, although it is usually referred to as the 'Isle of Harris'.

The Gaelic name for Harris is *Na Hearadh*. However, the name actually comes from the Norse *Haerri* meaning 'higher island' – Harris has more high hills than Lewis to the north – which was anglicized to 'Harris'. The name is quite unrelated to the common English and Welsh surnames Harris and Harrison; those derive from the personal name Henry.

But it was the island that lent its name to the world-famous Harris Tweed, which was hand-woven there from the 19th century onwards. It is something of a curiosity that Harris Tweed takes its name from two Scottish places at completely opposite ends of the country.

Hawick

Town in the Borders famous for knitwear and rugby. The name comes from two Old English words, *haga* meaning 'hedge' and *wic* meaning 'settlement', giving us 'hedge settlement'. Famous people from Hawick include rugby commentator Bill McLaren.

Hebrides

Group of islands off the north-west coast of Scotland. The islands are divided into the Outer and Inner Hebrides, and include Lewis and Harris, Skye, Mull,

Barra, North and South Uist, Jura, Islay, and St Kilda, as well as many other famous Scottish islands. The Outer Hebrides are also known as 'The Western Isles'. Being the last remaining stronghold of the Gaelic language in Scotland, they are officially known by their Gaelic name *Na h-Eileanan Siar*, which is also the name of the local-government authority and parliamentary constituency that covers the area.

The English name 'Hebrides' is thought to originate from Roman historians who wrote of a group of islands called *Haebudes* (although there is no record of what that name meant). At some time after the 16th century, the Roman name was translated into English and the letters 'ri' replaced the 'u'. Another possible origin is from the Norse *Havbredey* meaning 'islands at the edge of the sea'.

In Gaelic the Hebrides are known as *Innse Gall* meaning 'islands of the foreigners', due to the islands being ruled from the 10th to the 13th century by the Norsemen as part of their huge sea kingdom. In the 14th and 15th centuries, the Hebrides, although nominally part of the kingdom of Scotland, were ruled by the 'Lords of The Isles', usually members of the Clan MacDonald.

The Hebrides Overture was a famous composition by Felix Mendelssohn, who had visited the islands, although it is today better known as *Fingal's Cave*.

Helensburgh

Town on the north shore of the Firth of Clyde. Helensburgh is both a wealthy commuter town serving Glasgow and a popular destination for tourists who wish to see the Hill House, designed by Charles Rennie Mackintosh, which is located there. Helensburgh was founded in 1776 by Sir James Colquhoun, who built the town along similar lines to Edinburgh's New Town, and named the town in honour of his wife, Lady Helen, Countess of Sutherland.

Famous people born in Helensburgh include John Logie Baird, the inventor of television, and Hollywood film star Deborah Kerr.

Holyrood

Historic area of Edinburgh. Holyrood sits at the foot of Edinburgh's Royal Mile and is the site of both a royal palace and the Scottish Parliament. The now ruined Holyrood Abbey was built in the 12th century and the Palace of Holyroodhouse was built in the early 16th century in the reigns of James IV and James V. Mary, Queen of Scots lived there, although her time in the palace was not always happy – her servant David Rizzio was murdered in front of her in 1565. The Palace of Holyroodhouse remains an official royal residence of the British monarch, and the Queen stays there for one week a year. The nearby Holyrood Park is also owned by the Crown, but is open to the public and includes lochs, crags and Edinburgh's famous hill, Arthur's Seat, all just a mile away from the centre of Edinburgh.

Holyrood was controversially selected by Donald Dewar, then Secretary of State for Scotland, as the site of the new Scottish Parliament in 1998, but the building was only finished in 2004, several years late and somewhat over-budget, and with its Catalan architect Enric Miralles having died in 2000 before the project was completed. The Parliament was officially opened by the Queen, who was conveniently staying next door at the Palace, and so was able to get back home in time for her tea.

Holyrood was originally called 'Holy Rood' with *rood* being the Scots word for 'cross'. The name was given to the Abbey when it was founded in 1127 by King David I in thanks for having his life saved when out hunting in the nearby forest. Attempts have been made to revert to the original pronunciation of 'Holy Rood' (rather than the usual 'Holly Rood'), but these have on the whole proved unsuccessful.

Houston

Historic village in Renfrewshire. The village gives its name to the Scottish surname of Houston and thus indirectly to the city of Houston in Texas, which has a population of over 2,000,000 and is the fourth-largest city in the United States.

The original village was named after a 12th-century Norman landowner, Hugh de Padinan, and the name means 'Hugh's town'. The American city was founded in 1836 at a time when Texas was briefly an independent country (it only joined the United States in 1845) and was named after the then President of Texas, Samuel Houston.

The famous expression 'Houston, we have a problem' does not refer to American singer Whitney Houston, but to Mission Control at the NASA Space Centre in Houston. In 1970, the year after the first moon landings, the *Apollo XIII* mission to the moon suffered a serious explosion and had to be abandoned. The world watched breathlessly to see if the astronauts on the spacecraft would make it safely back to Earth. As it turned out, they did, and so the film *Apollo 13* would have a happy ending. In fact, the phrase popularly associated with this episode is a misquotation: what astronaut Jim Lovell actually said was the slightly less memorable 'Houston, we've had a problem.'

Hoy

The second-largest and highest island in Orkney. Hoy was the site of the main naval base for Scapa Flow in the Second World War, and The Old Man of Hoy is a famous 450-feet tall sea stack that was first climbed only in 1966. The name 'Hoy' derives from the Norse word *haey* and means 'high island'. Hoy is also a Scottish surname, and famous Hoys include Scottish Olympic gold-medal winning cyclist Chris Hoy.

Huntly

Town in Aberdeenshire. Huntly was a historic stronghold of the Earls of Huntly and is the site of the ruined 13th-century Huntly Castle. Huntly is associated with the Gordon family and the name 'Huntly' was originally a Borders place name that the Gordons (originally a Borders family) took north with them, first as the name of the castle, and then for the town when it was built in the 18th century. The name derives from the Old English *hunta leah* and means 'hunter's wood'.

Inveraray

Town on Loch Fyne in Argyll. Inveraray was built in the 18th century around Inveraray Castle, the family seat of the chief of the Clan Campbell and Duke of Argyll. The 19th-century Inveraray Jail has become an unlikely tourist destination. The name 'Inveraray' derives from the Gaelic *inbhir* meaning 'mouth of the river' and *Aray* the name of the river that enters the loch there.

Inverclyde

Local-authority area to the west of Glasgow.
'Inverclyde' means 'the mouth of the Clyde' with *Inver*
deriving from the Gaelic *inbhir* meaning 'mouth of
the river', although as Inverclyde is a region rather
than a town, the use of this term is not strictly correct.

Invergordon

Highland town and port in Easter Ross on the
Cromarty Firth. Invergordon was a base for the Royal
Navy until 1956 and is currently the location for
oil-rig repairs. The name 'Invergordon' was adopted in
honour of the town's founder, Alexander Gordon, in
the 18th century, and there is in fact no River Gordon
for the town to be at 'the mouth of'.

Inverkeithing

Town and port on Firth of Forth in Fife. Inverkeithing
is best known for being a stopping point for rail
services heading north from Edinburgh. The name
means 'the mouth of the Keithing Burn', deriving
from *inbhir* meaning 'mouth of the river'. The
Keithing Burn possibly takes its name from the
Brythonic word *coit* meaning 'wood', which would
give it the same derivation as the place name and
personal name Keith.

Inverness

The capital and administrative centre of the Highlands. Inverness became Scotland's fifth city in 2000. *Inver* comes from the Gaelic word *inbhir* meaning 'mouth of the river' and *Ness* from the River Ness (or *Nis* in Gaelic), whose original meaning is unknown. Residents of Inverness are called Invernesians, and famous people born there include Charles Kennedy, deposed leader of the Liberal Democrats. Inverness also features in Shakespeare's *Macbeth* when King Duncan is murdered at Inverness Castle in another act of political treachery.

Inverurie

Historic town in Aberdeenshire. The town is located to the north of Aberdeen at the place where the River Ury meets the River Don. The name 'Inverurie' means 'mouth of the Ury' with *Inver* deriving from the Gaelic *inbhir*. Inverurie was formerly 'Inverury', but the spelling was changed to help differentiate the town from Inveraray in Argyll.

Iona

Small island off the Isle of Mull in the Inner Hebrides. Iona has been a spiritual centre from the time when Saint Columba established the first monastery there in

563. It later became a place of pilgrimage and learning, and over 40 of Scotland's earliest kings were buried there, as was Labour leader John Smith in 1994.

The Gaelic name for the island is *Chalium Cille* which translates as 'Saint Columba's Island'. The English name 'Iona' comes from the Norse *ey* meaning 'island' possibly combined with an Irish word *eo* meaning 'the yew tree' (yews having a long association with churches).

Iona has also recently become a popular Scottish girls' name.

Irvine

Town in Ayrshire. Irvine had been a port from the 14th century, but was selected in the 1960s to be developed as a new town. Famous people born in Irvine include two politicians of differing persuasions in Jack McConnell and Nicola Sturgeon.

Irvine takes its name from the River Irvine. The name is possibly of Brythonic origin, with *wyn* meaning 'white river', or it may come from the Gaelic *odhar* meaning 'brown river'.

A much larger Irvine is to be found in Orange County, California. That city has a population of over 200,000 people and was named after a family of landowners called Irvine who had emigrated to

America from Belfast.

Irvine has also become a common Scottish surname, and occasionally a first name – as in the case of *Trainspotting* author Irvine Welsh.

Islay

Most southerly island of the Inner Hebrides and fifth-largest of the Scottish islands. Islay is today world famous for its whisky distilleries with seven distilleries currently operating on the island, including the famous malts Bowmore, Lagavulin, and Laphroaig. Islay was also famous in Scottish history for being the power-base for centuries for the mighty Clan MacDonald of the Isles. In the 14th and 15th centuries the MacDonalds were also the Lords of the Isles and ruled the whole of the Hebrides from Islay. Famous people born in Islay include Secretary-General of NATO George Robertson.

The name 'Islay' is of Norse origin. The ending comes from *ey* meaning 'island', but the meaning of the first syllable is unclear. It may possibly be from a Norse personal name *Yula*.

Jarlshof

Prehistoric settlement at the southern end of the Mainland of Shetland. The settlement dates from

2500BC and, remarkably, shows evidence of human habitation in the same location through the Iron Age, the Bronze Age, the Pictish and Viking eras, right through to the 16th century.

The name 'Jarlshof' was first used by author Sir Walter Scott, who visited the Old House of Sumburgh in 1814 and gave it this name (which is Norse for 'Earl's mansion') in his novel *The Pirate*. When a severe storm unearthed the location's ancient buildings later in the 19th century, the name Jarlshof was used for the site, although the name of Sumburgh remains in use for the nearby village and for Shetland's main airport.

Jedburgh

Historic town in the Borders. Jedburgh is best known for its ruined 12th-century abbey. The town is built on the Jed Water, from which it gets its name, although locals call the town 'Jeddart' or 'Jethart'. The term 'Jeddart Justice' refers to hanging a man first and then trying him for the crime later (no longer an official policy). Famous people born in Jedburgh include David Brewster, the inventor of the kaleidoscope.

John o' Groats

Village on the Caithness coast. Although it is not technically the most northerly settlement on the Scottish and British mainland (nearby Dunnet having that honour), the village is famous for its position at the extremity of the British mainland, and travelling from John o' Groats to Land's End in Cornwall is the accepted route for crossing Britain from top to bottom. The most famous attraction at John o' Groats is the signpost there that says 'Journey's End'.

John o' Groats takes its name from a Dutchman, Jan de Groot, who was given a grant in 1496 to run a ferry from the mainland to Orkney.

Johnstone

Town in Renfrewshire. Johnstone was mainly built in the 18th century, although the place name goes back to medieval times. The name means 'John's settlement'. Famous people born in Johnstone include television chef Gordon Ramsay, although it has to be said that not everybody from Johnstone has quite the same propensity for swearing.

Johnstone is also a popular Scottish surname, a variation of the more common Johnston, which means 'son of John', although some Johnstones will have taken their surname from the town. Famous

Johnstones include former Celtic footballer Jimmy 'Jinky' Johnstone.

Jura

Island in the Inner Hebrides, north of Islay. Jura is best known for producing Isle of Jura malt whisky and for author George Orwell having lived on the island for three years. The name 'Jura' derives from the Norse *dyr ey* and means 'deer island'.

Keith

Town in the north-east of Scotland. The name 'Keith' either derives from the Pictish first name *Cait* or the Brythonic *coit* meaning 'wood'. Keith has become a common surname and boys' first name, with famous Keiths including indestructible Rolling Stones guitarist Keith Richards and the less than indestructible drummer with The Who, the late Keith Moon.

Kelso

Town in the Borders. The picturesque market town was built around the long-ruined 12th-century Kelso Abbey and a bridge that crossed the River Tweed.

The name 'Kelso' derives from the Old English *calc how* and means 'chalk hill'. The earliest settlement was believed to have been built on a chalky outcrop.

Kelvin

River that runs through the west end of Glasgow. The area around the Kelvin became known as Kelvinside and became the home of Glasgow University in the 19th century. Other prominent buildings in the area include the Kelvingrove Art Gallery and Museum, the most visited attraction in Scotland, and the athletics stadium Kelvin Hall. Kelvinside is known as being one of the most affluent areas of Glasgow and the Kelvinside accent is said to be somewhat refined.

Eminent physicist William Thomson was a professor at Glasgow University in the 19th century and was ennobled as Lord Kelvin. The scale of absolute temperature that he invented was called the Kelvin scale in his honour, and the Kelvin is the SI unit of thermodynamic temperature.

Kelvin has also become a male first name and famous Kelvins include Kelvin MacKenzie, who despite his name is an English journalist and an outspoken critic of all things Scottish.

The name 'Kelvin' derives from the Gaelic *caol abhainn* meaning 'narrow river'. Strathkelvin is the name of a former local-government district in the Strathclyde region and means 'valley of the Kelvin'.

Killin

Village at the west end of Loch Tay in Stirling. Killin is a popular tourist destination, its most famous attraction being the Falls of Dochart. Despite its violent sounding name, Killin actually comes from the Gaelic *cill fionn* and means 'white church'.

Kilmarnock

Administrative centre of East Ayrshire. The first ever collection of Robert Burns' poetry was published here and was called *The Kilmarnock Edition*. The town is also known for being the home of Johnnie Walker whisky, first sold in Kilmarnock in 1820, and now the most widely distributed blended whisky in the world. The name 'Kilmarnock' comes from *kil*, the Gaelic word for a small Celtic church, and the 5th-century Saint Marnoch. Kilmarnock is often shortened to 'Killie'.

Kilwinning

Historic town in North Ayrshire. Kilwinning is the location of a ruined 12th-century abbey and the name has a Christian origin, with *kil* being the Gaelic for 'Celtic church' and *Winning* being derived from either the 6th-century Irish Saint Finian (who taught Saint Columba) or a later and more obscure 8th-century

Scottish saint called Winin. Famous people associated with Kilwinning include Bernard de Linton, the man who is believed to have written the most famous document in Scottish history – the 1320 Declaration of Arbroath. De Linton, who was abbot at Kilwinning before he moved to Arbroath, is buried at the abbey.

Kinross

Town in Perth and Kinross and former county town of Kinross-shire. Scotland's largest annual music festival, T in the Park, is held nearby. The name 'Kinross' derives from the Gaelic name *Ceann ros*, with *ceann* meaning 'head' and *ros* meaning 'promontory'.

Kintyre

Peninsula in western Scotland that divides the Atlantic Ocean from the Firth of Clyde. The name derives from the Gaelic *ceann* meaning 'head' and *tire* meaning 'of the land'. Paul McCartney, when he was a Wing rather than a Beatle, lived on a farm at the Mull of Kintyre ('Mull' meaning 'headland') at the southern tip of the peninsula and commemorated the place in a chart-topping single in 1977.

Kirkcaldy

Largest town in Fife. Kirkcaldy is also known as 'The Lang Toun' because of the length of its main street. Kirkcaldy does not take its name from the Scots word *kirk* meaning 'church', but rather from the Brythonic words *caer* (meaning 'fort'), *caled* (meaning 'hard') and *din* (meaning 'hill'), which means the town's name may be translated as 'fort on the hard hill'.

Famous people born in Kirkcaldy include architect Robert Adam, former Liberal leader David Steel, renowned economist Adam Smith, and British Prime Minister Gordon Brown (whose renown as an economist remains to be decided).

Kirkcudbright

Town in Dumfries and Galloway and former county town of Kirkcudbrightshire. The name derives from either the Norse *Kirk Oobrie* or the Gaelic *Chille Cudbert*, both of which mean 'church of Cuthbert' in reference to Saint Cuthbert of Lindisfarne, whose remains were briefly interred in Kirkcudbright. Kirkcudbright is probably most famous for being one of the Scottish place names that visitors find most difficult to say, as none its component parts of 'kirk', 'cud', and 'bright' are heard in the correct pronunciation of 'kir-coo-bree'.

Kirkintilloch

Administrative centre of East Dunbartonshire. The town lies ten miles north of Glasgow and developed through the construction of the Forth and Clyde canal. It now promotes itself as the 'Canal Capital of Scotland'. Kirkintilloch does not take its name from the Scots word *kirk* meaning 'church', but from the Brythonic *caer* meaning 'fort' and the Gaelic *cinn tulaich* meaning 'at the head of the hill'.

Kirkwall

Capital, largest town, and administrative centre of Orkney. Kirkwall was the seat of the Norse rulers of the Northern Isles from the 9th century until the 13th century, and it was the Norsemen who built the town's magnificent Saint Magnus Cathedral in memory of the martyred Magnus, Earl of Orkney. The name 'Kirkwall' comes from the Norse *kirkjuvagr* meaning 'church bay', which first became 'Kirkvoe' and then 'Kirkwaa' before being mistakenly translated into English as Kirkwall.

Kirriemuir

Market town in Angus. Kirriemuir is best known for being the birthplace of *Peter Pan* author J.M. Barrie, who called the town 'Thrums' in many of his novels.

Other famous people born in Kirriemuir include Bon Scott, original singer with Australian rock band AC/DC. Film star David Niven claimed to have been born in Kirriemuir, but was in fact born in London.

The name 'Kirriemuir' is derived from the Gaelic *ceathhramh* that means 'quarter', an old Scots term for a measure of land, and *muir*, which is either the Scots for 'moor' or comes from the Gaelic *mor* meaning 'great'. Kirriemuir is often shortened by locals to 'Kirrie'.

Kyle

Name that occurs in several Scottish locations, the most famous being the Ayrshire district of Kyle and the Highland village of Kyle of Lochalsh.

Kyle of Lochalsh lies at the mainland end of the Skye Bridge and is the final stop on the picturesque Inverness to Kyle of Lochalsh railway line. The name 'Kyle' comes from the Gaelic word *caol* meaning either 'strait' or 'channel'.

Kyle has become a common surname in both Scotland and Ireland, and has recently become a popular male first name. Famous Kyles include actor Kyle MacClachlan and daytime-television presenter Jeremy Kyle.

Lanark

Historic town that first became a royal burgh in the 12th century, and gives its name to the greater Lanarkshire area. It was in Lanark that William Wallace began his campaign of resistance by killing the town's English sheriff in 1297. Lanark is also the birthplace of football manager Walter Smith and world rallying champion Colin McRae. Lanark takes its name from the Brythonic word *llanerch* meaning 'forest clearing'. *Lanark* is also the name of a famous novel by Scottish writer Alasdair Gray.

The historic county of Lanarkshire is now divided between the local-government authorities of North Lanarkshire and South Lanarkshire. The area was historically known as a heartland of the Scottish coalmining industry, and remains (just) a heartland of the Scottish Labour Party.

Langholm

Town in Dumfries and Galloway. The name 'Langholm' derives from the Scots word *lang* meaning 'long' and *holm*, which probably derives from the Norse word *holmr* meaning either 'water meadow' or 'dry land' – although locals call the place 'The Muckle Toon' ('the large town'). Famous people born in Langholm include poet Hugh MacDiarmid, while engineer Thomas Telford was born nearby.

Largs

Seaside resort in North Ayrshire. The Battle of Largs in 1263 is one of the most famous battles in Scottish history. It was fought between Scotland and Norway and marked the end of Norwegian rule over the Western Isles (although nobody is sure who actually won the battle). Famous people born in Largs include golfer Sam Torrance and actress Daniela Nardini, whose family are prominent local ice-cream entrepreneurs. The name 'Largs' derives from the Gaelic *leargaidh* and means 'hill-slope' or 'hillside'.

Lauder

Town in the Borders. Lauder lies on the Leader Water, from which it takes its name. The valley of the Leader Water is known as Lauderdale.

Lauder is also a Scottish surname and famous Lauders include entertainer Harry Lauder, who became famous around the world for songs such as 'Keep Right On to the End of the Road'.

An even more famous holder of the name is the international cosmetics company Estee Lauder, which sells over 70 perfumes around the world. The company was founded in New York in 1946 by Estee Lauder, who was born Josephine Esther Mentzer before she married one Joseph Lauter and the couple changed their surname to Lauder.

Laurencekirk

Small town in Aberdeenshire and largest settlement in The Mearns. Laurencekirk takes its name from a parish called Kirkton of St Laurence, named after the Christian saint. In the late 18th century this parish was amalgamated with another parish called Conveth to form a single village, and Laurencekirk became the name of the new community.

Leith

Historic port of Edinburgh that was a separate town until 1920. Leith was twice sacked by the English in the 1540s, was the garrison for the French soldiers who supported the Scottish crown in the 1550s, and it was here that Mary, Queen of Scots returned to Scotland in 1561. After a period of decline Leith has seen much recent development with the headquarters of the Scottish Government and the Royal Yacht Britannia being located there. Local author Irvine Welsh set most of his novel *Trainspotting* in Leith, and Scottish band The Proclaimers had a bestselling album called *Sunshine on Leith*. Leith is also noted for being the home of Hibernian Football Club and of the computer-game company Rockstar North, developers of *Grand Theft Auto*.

The name 'Leith' possibly derives from a Brythonic word *lleith* meaning 'wet place', presumably a reference to the weather rather than any other activities.

The Water of Leith is a river that runs from the Pentland Hills through Edinburgh and flows into the Firth of Forth at Leith. Its banks are a popular walking route.

Lerwick

Capital, largest town and administrative centre of Shetland. Lerwick is the most northerly town in the United Kingdom and historically was an important fishing port. It is known for hosting the annual Viking midwinter festival of Up-Helly-Aa. The name 'Lerwick' is appropriately Norse and comes from the words *leir vik* meaning 'muddy bay'.

Lesmahagow

Small town in South Lanarkshire. The name 'Lesmahagow' is of uncertain origin. It may possibly derive from the Gaelic *lios* meaning 'enclosure', with *mahagow* referring to a 6th-century Welsh saint called Machutus (or Saint Malo) to whom the now-ruined Lesmahagow Priory was dedicated.

Leven

Name of several places in Scotland. The name 'Leven' appears to have the same meaning in each case, deriving from the Gaelic *leamhain* meaning 'elms' or 'water by the elms'.

In Perth and Kinross, a Loch Leven is the location for the ruined Lochleven Castle, from where Mary, Queen of Scots made a dramatic escape from imprisonment in 1568. The loch is the source of the River Leven that flows through Fife and enters the Firth of Forth at the town of Leven.

In the Highlands another River Leven flows into another Loch Leven at the village Kinlochleven.

And in West Dunbartonshire, yet another River Leven flows from Loch Lomond to Dumbarton on the Firth of Clyde. The area around the this river is known as the Vale of Leven, with the English word *vale* uncharacteristically preferred to the Gaelic word *strath* to refer to a wide valley.

Lewis

Northern part of the island of Lewis and Harris in the Outer Hebrides. Lewis and Harris is the largest Scottish island both in terms of population and geographical area.

The Gaelic name for Lewis is *Eileann Leodhas* and so it is often thought that the name comes from the Gaelic *leoghuis* meaning 'marshy'. It is more probable, however, that the name derives from the Old Norse *ljodhus* meaning 'homes of the people'. The anglicized name of the island is unconnected with the English and Welsh personal name Lewis – that derives from the French name *Louis*. However, Lewis is currently the most popular boys' name in Scotland, and these latter-day Lewises are predominantly named after the Hebridean island. Famous Scots called Lewis include Lewis Grassic Gibbon, author of classic novel *Sunset Song*.

The Lewis Chessmen are a collection of 95 chess pieces dating from the 12th century that were discovered on Lewis in 1831. They are now on display partly in the British Museum in London and partly in the National Museum of Scotland in Edinburgh, which makes it quite difficult to play a game.

Linlithgow

Historic town and popular tourist location in West Lothian. The town is the location of Linlithgow Palace, built in the 15th century, but lacking a roof since 1746. The name derives from the Brythonic *llyn lleith cau* meaning 'the lake in the wet hollow'. Residents of Linlithgow are known as 'Black Bitches', due to the town's crest featuring a black female dog tied to a tree on an island, a reference to the legend of a faithful dog who would bring food to her imprisoned master and was tied up by the authorities to stop her from doing so.

Famous people born in Linlithgow include James V of Scotland, Mary, Queen of Scots, Scotland's First Minister Alex Salmond, and Chief Engineer Montgomery Scott of the *Starship Enterprise*, who is due to be born there in 2222.

Linwood

Former industrial town in Renfrewshire. Linwood was noted for car production before its plant closed in 1981. The name probably derives from an Old English word *lind* meaning 'lime tree'.

Livingston

New town in West Lothian, established in 1962. Livingston took its name from the old village of Livingston, which in turn was named either after a 12th-century Flemish merchant called De Leving or else after an earlier English landowner called Leving.

Lochaber

Mountainous region in the western Highlands. Lochaber gives its name to the Lochaber axe, a long battle-axe that was used to hook riders off their horses. The name 'Lochaber' combines the Gaelic world *loch* with the Brythonic word *aber* meaning 'where the waters meet', a reference to the many lochs in the area – although it is possible that in this case *aber* might have a different meaning. 'Lochaber No More' is the name of a traditional Scots lament and is also the last line of The Proclaimers' first hit record, 'Letter from America'.

Lochalsh

District in Wester Ross directly opposite the Isle of Skye. Lochalsh takes its name from Loch Alsh, the sea loch which lies between Skye and the mainland. The origin of the name *Alsh* is unknown but possibly means 'foaming'.

Kyle of Lochalsh ('Kyle' meaning 'strait') is the main village of Lochalsh and connects the Scottish mainland to the Isle of Skye through the 1995 Skye Bridge.

Loch Fyne

Sea loch in Argyll. This long stretch of water is famous for fishing and especially for its oysters. Loch Fyne Oysters and Restaurants is a seafood chain that takes its name from the sea loch and the first Oyster Bar was opened at the loch in 1988. The name of the loch comes from the River Fyne, one of the streams that run into it, and which may derive from the Gaelic word *fine* meaning 'wine'. If this is true, it is quite appropriate, as wine and oysters do go rather well together.

Lochgilphead

Administrative centre of Argyll and Bute.
Lochgilphead was built in 1790 to coincide with the building of the road from Inveraray to Campbeltown. The name means what it says, as the town as is at the head of Loch Gilp, an inlet of the larger Loch Fyne.

Lochinver

Fishing village on the west coast of Sutherland at the head of Loch Inver. Lochinver is dominated by the mountain Suilven which stands behind the village. The name means 'loch at the river mouth', with *Inver* deriving from the Gaelic *inbhir*.

The slightly different name Lochinvar was made famous by the romantic 'young Lochinvar' in the poem by Sir Walter Scott. This character was named after a loch in Dumfries and Galloway whose name means 'loch on the hilltop', from the Gaelic *loch an barr*.

Loch Katrine

Freshwater loch in the Trossachs that is the main reservoir serving Glasgow. Loch Katrine is a popular tourist destination and is the 'lake' in Sir Walter Scott's novel *The Lady of the Lake*. The name 'Katrine' does not come from the same origin as the Scottish girls' name Catriona, but either derives from the Brythonic word *cethern* meaning 'furies' or the Gaelic *cateran* meaning 'Highland robber' (a highly appropriate name, as Rob Roy Macgregor was born at the head of the loch).

Loch Linnhe

Sea loch on the west coast of Scotland that has Fort William at its north-eastern end. The name 'Linnhe' derives from the Gaelic *linne* meaning 'pool'. In Gaelic, the inner loch is known as *An Linne Dhubh* ('the dark pool'), while the outer loch is known as *An Linne Sheileach* ('the salty pool').

Loch Lomond

Freshwater loch north of Glasgow. In terms of surface area, Loch Lomond is both the largest loch in Scotland and the largest area of inland water in Britain. It has long been a popular tourist destination and in 2002 became part of the Loch Lomond and Trossachs National Park. Among the attractions on offer are water-sports, boat trips, and the Loch Lomond Golf Course. The origin of the word 'Lomond' is not known, but if it has the same

meaning as nearby Ben Lomond then it might come from the Gaelic *laomuinn* meaning 'beacon'.

The song 'Loch Lomond' is one Scotland's most famous and includes the lines:

> *Oh, ye'll take the high road, and I'll take the low road*
> *And I'll be in Scotland afore ye.*
> *But me and my true love will never meet again*
> *On the bonny, bonny banks of Loch Lomond.*

Currently, the main road to Loch Lomond is the A82.

Loch Ness

Freshwater loch in the Highlands. Loch Ness is the second-largest loch in Scotland by surface area and largest in volume. It runs south from Inverness and makes up part of the Caledonian Canal, forming one of Scotland's most popular tourist attractions, with Urquhart Castle on its north shore, Boleskine House (home at different times to occultist Aleister Crowley and Led Zeppelin guitarist Jimmy Page) on its south shore, and a certain large monster reputed to reside in its very deep waters.

The Loch Ness Monster (or 'Nessie' to her friends) was first recorded in the 6th century when Saint Columba is said to have had an altercation with the creature. From this time onwards Nessie has kept herself to herself and, other than a spate of sightings in the 1930s, has remained stubbornly elusive in spite of the thousands of visitors who travel to the Loch hoping to catch a glimpse.

The loch's name comes from the Gaelic name *Nis*, which is of unknown derivation, and is also found in the names of Inverness and the River Ness.

Loch Tay

Freshwater loch in Perthshire. Loch Tay is the sixth-largest loch in Scotland, with Ben Lawers on its northern shore. As with the River Tay, the origin of the name is unknown.

Lockerbie

Historic market town in Dumfries and Galloway. Lockerbie achieved a tragic notoriety in 1988 when an aeroplane exploded above the town, killing all its 259 passengers as well as 11 Lockerbie residents. The subsequent investigation, trial, and appeals by the convicted men have all helped to keep the name of Lockerbie in the public consciousness.

The name 'Lockerbie' does not derive from the word *loch*, but from *Locard*, the personal name of a Norse settler in the area. Thus 'Lockerbie' means 'Locard's village', with *bie* deriving from the Norse *by* meaning 'village' or 'settlement'. Locard would also give his name to the popular Scottish surname Lockhart.

Lossiemouth

Fishing port in Moray, originally the port for the town of Elgin. Lossiemouth was built where the River Lossie flows into the Moray Firth. The river was first recorded in a 2nd-century Roman map with the name of *Loxa*, which is believed to mean 'crooked'. Since 1939 Lossiemouth has been an important base for the Royal Air Force. Famous people born in Lossiemouth include the first British Labour Prime Minister, James Ramsay MacDonald.

Lothian

Region of Scotland south of the Firth of Forth. Lothian was an ancient kingdom of first the Britons and then, from the 7th century, the Angles. It was finally incorporated into the kingdom of Scotland in 1018, but remained the most Anglo-Saxon part of the kingdom with Gaelic never becoming the main language. In fact, it was the Lothian form of the English language that would become dominant in the Lowlands of Scotland and eventually the whole country. The name 'Lothian' is believed to derive from a legendary king variously known as Lot, Louth or Leudonus, who was the first King of Lothian and was said to be the brother-in-law of King Arthur.

Lothian is today divided into three local-government authorities: West Lothian, Midlothian and East Lothian.

Loudoun

District in East Ayrshire to the east of Kilmarnock. Robert the Bruce won a victory over the English at the Battle of Loudoun Hill in 1307, and Loudoun Castle is today the name of a popular family theme park.

The name 'Loudoun' is of uncertain origin. It has been suggested that it may derive from a Celtic god called *Lugh* or from the Gaelic words *loch* meaning 'lake' and *dun* meaning 'hill'. Loudoun County is also the name of a county in the state of Virginia, and John Loudon McAdam was the name of the Scottish engineer who revolutionized road-building.

Mallaig

Town and port in Lochaber in the western Highlands. Mallaig is the final stop on the West Highland Railway, the final stop on the A830 (better known as 'The Road to the Isles') and the departure point for ferries to Knoydart and many of the smaller Hebridean islands. It is also the main fishing port in the western Highlands. The name 'Mallaig' possibly derives from the Norse *muli vagr* meaning 'headland bay'.

Markinch

Small town in Fife, said to be the ancient capital of the Kingdom of Fife. The name 'Markinch' derives from the Gaelic words *marc* meaning 'horse' and *innes* meaning 'island' or 'meadow', as it is said that the original settlement was built on an island in a lake that was later drained.

Maryhill

Area of Glasgow. Maryhill was formerly a separate town, but became part of the City of Glasgow in 1891. It was developed in the 19th century in conjunction with the Forth and Clyde Canal that flows through it. The name was chosen by local landowner Robert Graham, who sold part of the estate of Gairbraid for development in the 1780s on the condition that any future town on this land would be named after his wife, Mary Hill, who had inherited the Gairbraid estate from her father.

Today, Maryhill is known throughout the world as the location for the television series *Taggart*.

Mauchline

Town in East Ayrshire. Mauchline is best known for being the setting for many of the poems of Robert Burns, who lived on a farm on the outskirts of the town. William Fisher, an elder of the Mauchline Kirk, was satirized in Burns' poem 'Holy Willie's Prayer', and Jean Armour, the poet's long-suffering wife, was born in the town.

The origin of the name 'Mauchline' is either from the Gaelic *magh* meaning 'field' or 'plain' and *linne* meaning 'pool', or else from *Macha Ruad*, the legendary High Queen of Ireland and goddess.

Mearns

Name of a region in Kincardineshire and also a district south of Glasgow. The name is believed to derive from the Gaelic *merrns* meaning 'stewardship', the equivalent of the Scots word 'Stewartry'.

The Kincardineshire Mearns is farming country and was made famous by author Lewis Grassic Gibbon as the setting of his classic novel *Sunset Song*, the first book in the trilogy *A Scots Quair*.

The town of Newton Mearns was built in the 19th century and has become a popular commuter town serving Glasgow.

Melrose

Historic town and tourist destination in the Borders. Melrose is famous for the ruined 12th-century Melrose Abbey, where the heart of King Robert the

Bruce is buried. The town is overlooked by the Eildon Hills where, according to legend, King Arthur lies sleeping, and nearby Abbotsford was the home of Sir Walter Scott. Melrose is also the place where rugby sevens, the abbreviated form of rugby union, was first played in 1883, and the town hosts the annual Melrose Sevens tournament.

The name 'Melrose' derives from the Brythonic and either means 'bare promontory' (from the words *mail* meaning 'bare' and *ros* meaning 'promontory'), or 'bare meadow' (if the second part comes from *rhos* meaning 'meadow').

Melrose Place was a popular 1990s American television series, named after the fashionable district of Melrose in the West Hollywood area of the Los Angeles.

Menteith

Historic district and earldom in Perthshire between the rivers Teith and Forth. Menteith is most notable for its Lake of Menteith, the only major body of water in Scotland that has the English word 'lake' rather than the Scottish 'loch' in its name. Rather than a deliberate attempt at anglicization, however, this is in fact an accidental variation of the Scots *laich o' Menteith*, with *laich* being a Scots word meaning 'low ground'.

The name 'Menteith' is of ancient Pictish origin its meaning is uncertain. One suggestion is that it means simply 'land of the river Teith'.

Midlothian

Region and local-government authority south of Edinburgh. Together with East Lothian and West Lothian, it is one of the three divisions of the ancient kingdom of Lothian. The city of Edinburgh itself was part of Midlothian until 1929, but is now governed by a separate authority.

The name 'Heart of Midlothian' was first given to the old Tolbooth prison in Edinburgh, and was the name of an 1818 novel by Sir Walter Scott that was set in the city. The Tolbooth was demolished in the 19th century, but a heart-shaped mosaic marks the place on the Royal Mile where it used to be. There is a local tradition that passers-by should spit on the mosaic, although the reason for this is disputed. Heart of Midlothian Football Club, more affectionately known as Hearts or 'the Jam Tarts', was founded in Edinburgh in 1874 and has won the Scottish League championship four times, but not since 1960.

Milngavie

Commuter town to the north of Glasgow in East
Dunbartonshire. Milngavie is the starting point
of the West Highland Way. The name 'Milngavie'
derives from *muileann* the Gaelic word for 'mill', but
it is unclear whether the mill in question belonged
to someone called Gavin or someone called David.
Today, Milngavie is pronounced 'mill-guy', with the
'v' silent, which was perhaps a compromise, refusing
to give either Gavin or David the honour of being the
person after whom the town was named.

Moffat

Small town and spa resort in Dumfries and Galloway.
The name 'Moffat' possibly derives from the Gaelic
magh meaning 'plain' and *fada* meaning 'long'. Moffat
is also a Scottish surname, and famous Moffats
include *Doctor Who* producer Steven Moffat.

Monklands

District in North Lanarkshire. Monklands includes
the towns of Airdrie and Coatbridge and was the
name of a former local-government district and two
parliamentary constituencies, with Monklands East
being the seat of Labour leader John Smith. The
name 'Monklands' derives from the parishes of Old

and New Monklands, which were established on land given to Cistercian monks by King Malcolm IV in the 12th century.

Montrose

Historic town and port in Angus. Montrose probably takes its name from the former Rossie Island that is now part of Montrose harbour, with 'Rossie' deriving from the Norse word *hrossay* meaning 'horse island'. (Alternatively, the name could derive from the Gaelic *moine* meaning 'peat' or 'moss' and *ros* meaning 'headland' or 'promontory'.) Montrose is famous for James Graham, the 1st Marquis of Montrose, who led the Royalists in Scotland in the Civil Wars of the 1640s.

Moray

Local-government area and former county in north-east Scotland. Moray was one of the original mormaerdoms or minor kingdoms and later earldoms of Scotland. The name 'Moray' comes from the Gaelic word *moraibh* meaning 'sea settlement'. From the place name Moray we also get the male first name Moray or Murray, the surname Murray, and the popular sweet Murray Mints.

The Moray Firth is the 500-mile long area of the

North Sea that extends from Inverness up to John o' Groats in the north and Fraserburgh in the east and is Scotland's largest coastal inlet. (*Firth* is a Scots word for 'coastal waters' and is similar to the Scandinavian word *fjord*.) The Moray Firth is the best place in Scotland for observing dolphins, porpoises and whales.

Morningside

Suburb of south-west Edinburgh. The affluent suburb of Morningside is known for the refined speech of its residents. The heroine of Muriel Spark's novel *The Prime of Miss Jean Brodie* lived in Morningside, and the area is often associated with its genteel ladies, although men do reside there as well. Famous examples of the Morningside accent include 'sex' being what you put the coal in, and a 'creche' being a road accent. Others have said sneeringly about the ladies of Morningside that they are 'all fur coats and nae knickers', a remark that is surely unfounded, as no Morningside local would ever say 'nae'.

The origins of the name 'Morningside' are unclear, but it is possible that it derives from the phrase 'the morning side', in recognition of a farm in the area that received more than its share of morning sunshine.

Motherwell

Administrative centre of North Lanarkshire.
Motherwell was at the forefront of Scotland's steel
industry until the 1980s and their football team is
nicknamed 'the Steelmen'. The name comes from a
well that was dedicated to the Virgin Mary.

Muckle Flugga

Uninhabited island north of Shetland. Muckle Flugga
is traditionally considered the most northerly point
of Britain (although technically the nearby outcrop
of Out Stack is further north). In 1858 a lighthouse
was built on the island, which was formerly known as
North Unst. The name 'Muckle Flugga' comes from
the Shetland word *muckle* (derived from the Norse
mikla meaning 'big') and the Norse *flugey* meaning
'steep island'. Muckle Flugga lighthouse has been
automated since 1995, and lighthouse keepers no
longer reside on the island.

Mull

Island in the Inner Hebrides. The fourth-largest
Scottish island, Mull is a popular tourist destination
and was the location for the children's television
programme *Balamory*. The origin of the name is
unclear, with suggestions ranging from the Gaelic *meal*

meaning 'rounded hill', the Gaelic *maol* meaning 'bare summit', or the Norse *muli* meaning 'headland'.

Musselburgh

Coastal town in East Lothian on the outskirts of Edinburgh. There has been a settlement at Musselburgh since Roman times. Musselburgh earned its nickname of 'The Honest Toun' in the 14th century, when the townsfolk refused payment for looking after the ill Earl of Moray, and residents are still known as 'Honest Lads' and 'Honest Lasses'. The town used to be a fishing port, and the name 'Musselburgh' comes from the Old English *musle* meaning 'mussels' and *burgh* meaning 'town'.

Nairn

Coastal town in the Highland region. Nairn was formerly the county town of Nairnshire and is a popular tourist resort. Famous people born in Nairn include former Deputy Prime Minister William Whitelaw. Nairn takes its name from the River Nairn, but the origin of the river's name is unknown. Nairn is also a Scottish surname and famous Nairns include television chef Nick Nairn.

New Lanark

Model village in South Lanarkshire. The village took its name from the nearby historic town of Lanark, but has become famous in its own right for its preserved houses and cotton mills, built by David Dale and his socially reforming son-in-law Robert Owen in the 18th and 19th centuries. It is a popular tourist attraction and World Heritage Site.

Newtongrange

Former mining village in Midlothian and the location of the Scottish Mining Museum. The final part of the name relates to the Grange of nearby Newbattle Abbey, and the *Newton* is in reference to the older Prestongrange in East Lothian. Locals, however, refer to Newtongrange as 'Nitten'.

Newtonmore

Village in the Highlands. Newtonmore was built in the 19th century and is a popular destination for tourists and hill-walkers. It is also famous for its shinty team. The name 'Newtonmore' is English and self-explanatory, meaning 'new town on the moor'.

Newtown St Boswells

Administrative centre of the Scottish Borders. In spite
of its name, the place actually dates back to the 16th
century. The name 'St Boswells' is derived from the
7th-century Saint Boisil, who was abbot of nearby
Melrose Abbey.

Nith

River in south-west Scotland that rises in Ayrshire
and flows through Dumfries to the Solway Firth. The
name 'Nith' is believed to derive from the Brythonic
nedd meaning 'glistening'.

Nithsdale is the valley around the River Nith and a
district in Dumfries and Galloway.

North Berwick

Town in East Lothian. The town of North Berwick is
so called to differentiate it from Berwick-upon-Tweed
further to the south. North Berwick has become
famous for tourism, the 16th century North Berwick
witchcraft trials, and the Scottish Seabird Centre that
was opened in the town in 2000.

Oban

Town and tourist resort in Argyll and Bute. Oban
is known as 'The Gateway to the Isles', having

ferry connections to many of the Hebridean islands including Mull, Islay, and Barra. The novel and film *Morvern Callar* were set in Oban. The name comes from the Gaelic *An t-Oban* and means 'little bay'.

Ochils

Range of hills in central Scotland. The name 'Ochil' comes from a Brythonic word that, appropriately enough, means 'high'.

Orkney

Group of 67 islands (20 inhabited) off the north coast of Scotland. Orkney is famous for its ancient archaeological remains. The site of Skara Brae dates back to 3000BC, making it the oldest evidence of human settlement found in the United Kingdom, and Neolithic Orkney has become a World Heritage Site and popular tourist destination. Orkney was an important Viking earldom or 'jarldom' from the 9th century and was only ceded to Scotland from Norway in 1469. *The Orkneyinga Saga* was a 13th-century history telling the story of the early earls, including Saint Magnus, for whom Saint Magnus Cathedral was built. In both World Wars Orkney provided a major naval British base at Scapa Flow.

The people of Orkney are called Orcadians, and this

name harks back to a Roman geographer who referred to the islands as the *Orcades* in the 2nd century AD. The Gaelic name for the islands was *Insi Orc*, which means 'the island of the pigs', but when the Vikings arrived they changed the word *orc* to the Norse word *orkn* meaning 'seal' and called the islands *Orkneyjar* meaning 'seal islands'. That name was later shortened to give its current form. Famous Orcadians include the writer George Mackay Brown.

Paisley

Administrative centre of Renfrewshire. Paisley is the sixth-largest town or city in Scotland, with a population just less than that of East Kilbride. In the 19th century Paisley became known for the distinctive weaving of shawls using a pattern that originated in Iran and India. This pattern became hugely popular and was given the name of the 'Paisley pattern'. The pattern found new popularity in the 1960s and its rock-and-roll image was enhanced when Prince called his recording studio and record label Paisley Park.

Residents from Paisley refer to themselves as 'Buddies', a term that is believed to originate from the word 'bodies' used as a way of referring to people. The name 'Paisley' is thought to be of Brythonic origin, from the word *pasgell* that possibly means 'pasture' – a surprisingly serene meaning for a town that shares a surname with Northern Ireland politician Ian Paisley. Other famous Paisleys include former Liverpool football manager Bob Paisley.

Partick

District of Glasgow. Partick stands on the north bank of the River Clyde and was formerly a separate village before being incorporated into the city in 1912. The name 'Partick' is believed to originate from the Brythonic *perth* meaning 'thicket'. The football club Partick Thistle were formed in Partick in 1876, and have kept the name despite moving to Maryhill in the early 1900s.

Partick was also the location of the first ever football international when Scotland played England at Hamilton Crescent in 1872. The game ended 0-0, but there was no penalty shoot-out.

Peebles

Town in the Borders and former county town of Peebles-shire. The name derives from a Brythonic word *pebyll* meaning 'shielings' or 'sheds'. American singer Ann Peebles had a hit with 'I Can't Stand the Rain', although residents of Peebles are generally much more stoical about the weather.

Penicuik

Town in Midlothian. Until recently Penicuik was known for its paper mills. The name derives from the Brythonic *pen y cog* meaning 'hill of the cuckoo'.

Pennan

Former fishing village in Aberdeenshire near Fraserburgh. Pennan became world famous in 1983 as the picturesque location of the Bill Forsyth film *Local Hero*. The iconic red phonebox that featured in the film did not actually exist in the village before filming began, but a real phonebox was installed afterwards and has become a popular tourist destination. The name 'Pennan' is of uncertain origin but is possibly Pictish, with *pen* meaning 'hill' and *an* meaning 'stream' (as the village is at the foot of a steep headland).

Pentland

Name of two places in Scotland. The Pentland Hills lie to the south of Edinburgh and are popular with walkers. These take their name from the Brythonic word *pen* meaning 'hill'. At the opposite end of country, the Pentland Firth is the stretch of water between Orkney and the Scottish mainland, known for having some of the fastest tidal waters in the world. The Pentland Firth was previously known as the 'Pettland's Firth', a name derived from *Pettrland*, the Norse name for 'Pictland'.

Perth

Town in central Scotland, administrative centre of Perth and Kinross. Perth is one of Scotland's oldest royal burghs and was the capital of Scotland from the 12th century until 1437, when James I was murdered there. Perth is known as 'The Fair City', but in fact is no longer officially classed as a city (although a campaign is now underway to have the title restored). Perth is also known as 'Saint John's Toun' after the 15th-century Saint John's Kirk, and that name is still used today by the Perth football club St Johnstone. Famous people born in Perth include John Buchan, author of *The Thirty Nine Steps*. The name 'Perth' is believed to be a Pictish or Brythonic word meaning 'wood' or 'place of the thicket'.

A much larger Perth is the state capital of Western Australia. This has a population of over 1,500,000 and is Australia's fourth-largest city.

Peterhead

Fishing town in Aberdeenshire. In the 19th century Peterhead was a major centre of the herring industry, and it remains one of Europe's biggest white-fishing ports. Peterhead is nicknamed 'The Blue Toon' after the blue stockings that the local fishermen used to wear. The town was built in 1587 and took its name from a kirk dedicated to Saint Peter that stood on its headland.

Peterhead fishing skippers were the stars of *Trawlermen*, a television documentary series that had to be subtitled for both English and Scottish viewers so that they could understand the distinctive local Doric accent.

Pitlochry

Town in Perth and Kinross on the River Tummel. Now a popular destination for tourists and hill-walkers, Pitlochry developed in the 19th century after the coming of the railway. The name 'Pitlochry' does not derive from the word 'loch' but from the Gaelic *pit cloich aire*. *Pit* derives from the Pictish word *pett* meaning 'place', and the Gaelic *cloich aire* means 'sentinel stone'. This refers to a stone from which it is said that the ancient Picts would observe a nearby Roman fort for possible signs of attack.

Plockton

Picturesque village on the west Highland coast. Plockton lies on the shores of Loch Carron and is famous for its palm trees. It has been a popular film location and featured in both *The Wicker Man* and the television series *Hamish MacBeth*. The name derives from the Gaelic word *ploc* meaning 'lump' and the English word 'town'.

Pollok

Area of south-west Glasgow. It contains Pollok Country Park, which is home to the popular tourist attractions the Burrell Collection and Pollok House, as well the new Silverburn Shopping Centre.

The name 'Pollok' derives from the Brythonic *poll* meaning 'pool' and *oc* meaning 'little'. It also occurs in the names of two other areas in the south of Glasgow: Pollokshields (with *shields* being a Scots word for 'shielings' or 'summer pasture') and Pollokshaws (with *shaws* being a Scots word for 'woods').

The place name gives rise to the surname Pollock, and famous Pollocks include American painter Jackson Pollock and South African cricketers Graeme and Shaun Pollock.

Polmont

Town near Falkirk. Polmont is one of the stops on the train line between Edinburgh and Glasgow. The name derives from the Gaelic *poll* meaning 'pool' and *monadh* meaning 'hill'.

Portobello

Seaside resort on the Firth of Forth, incorporated into the city of Edinburgh in 1896. The name 'Portobello' derives from a cottage in the area that was named after a port in Panama called Puerto Bello, which means 'beautiful port' in Spanish, and was captured by the British in 1739 in a war with Spain. Portobello Road in London has the same origin. Famous people born in Portobello include singer and entertainer Harry Lauder.

Portpatrick

Village on the south-west extremity of the Scottish mainland. Portpatrick offers excellent views of the Irish coast and was the main port between Northern Ireland and Scotland until the 19th century. The name 'Portpatrick' honours this Irish connection, by being named after Saint Patrick, the patron saint of Ireland.

Portree

Main town on the Isle of Skye. The origin of the name 'Portree' is disputed. It is traditionally said that the name derives from the Gaelic words *port* meaning 'port' or 'harbour' and *right* meaning 'royal' or 'king', making Portree 'the king's port' in recognition of the visit to Skye by James V in 1540. However, another theory is that the *ree* derives from the Gaelic *ruighead* meaning 'slope', therefore making Portree 'the port of the slope'.

Prestwick

Town in South Ayrshire on the Firth of Clyde. Prestwick is famous for being the location for the first twelve Open Golf Championships (from 1860 onwards) and for Prestwick International Airport, first used in 1934 and for many years Scotland's only transatlantic airport. Elvis Presley changed planes here in 1960 when returning from military service in Germany – the only occasion he set foot on British soil. Prestwick Airport is officially called Glasgow Prestwick Airport, even though it is 30 miles away from Glasgow.

The name 'Prestwick' derives from the Old English *preost* meaning 'priest' and *wic* meaning 'farm'.

Princes Street

Street in the centre of Edinburgh. Princes Street is famous as Edinburgh's main shopping area, although one side of the street consists of the Princes Street Gardens. When plans were made to build the New Town area of Edinburgh in the late 18th century,

George Street was supposed to be the centrepiece of the development, but it was Princes Street, with its unobstructed views of Edinburgh Castle, that would become more prominent. The Princes Street Gardens were created in the 1820s when the Nor' Loch on the site was successfully drained. Subsequent developments on the street would include the Scott Monument in 1846, the Waverley train station in 1854, and the National Gallery of Scotland in 1859.

The original idea was to call the street 'St Giles Street' after Edinburgh's patron saint, but this was changed to a name more in keeping with the royal theme of the New Town, and 'Princes Street' was chosen in honour of the two eldest sons of King George III, Prince George and Prince Frederick. Prince George would later become King George IV and in 1822 would become the first monarch to visit to Scotland for nearly 200 years – although the visit would be mostly remembered for the king's unfortunate decision to wear an extremely short and unflattering kilt.

Princes Street and George Street are also the main street names in Dunedin in the South Island of New Zealand.

Queensferry

Name of two towns – North Queensferry and South Queensferry – on the Firth of Forth at either end of the Forth Bridge. The name 'Queensferry' honours the 11th-century Queen Margaret, wife of King Malcolm III (and later canonized as Saint Margaret), who regularly crossed the Forth at these points by ferry when travelling from the royal palace at Dunfermline to her chapel at Edinburgh Castle. The ferry here was also used by pilgrims from Lothian to cross over to Fife and travel on to St Andrews, the major religious centre of Scotland in the reign of Malcolm and Margaret.

Raasay

Scottish island to the east of Skye. Raasay has long been associated with the Clan MacLeod and famous people born there include poet Sorley MacLeod and crofter Calum MacLeod, about whom the book *Calum's Road* was written. The island's name derives from the Norse *Rarassey* and means 'roe-deer island'.

Rannoch

Area in central Highlands. Rannoch includes the boggy and somewhat bleak National Heritage site Rannoch Moor and Loch Rannoch in its west. The name comes from the Gaelic *Raineach* and means 'bracken'.

Renfrew

Historic town on the River Clyde west of Glasgow.
Renfrew gives its name to the local-government
authorities of Renfrewshire and East Renfrewshire.
The name is Brythonic, meaning 'point of the
current'.

Rest and Be Thankful

Popular viewing point at the summit of the pass
between Glen Croe and Loch Fyne. The name 'Rest
and Be Thankful' derives from an inscription left on a
stone by the soldiers who built the military road from
Dumbarton to Inveraray (now the A83) in the 1750s.
The stone no longer remains, but the inscription
became the name for the area, as is it is a long and
steep climb to the summit and one is thankful for
having finally got there.

Riccarton

Name of several places in the Lowlands. The name
means 'Richard's farm' with *Riccart* an Old English
form of the personal name Richard. The best-known
Riccarton is the site of the campus for Heriot-Watt
University in south-west Edinburgh.

Roslin

Village in Midlothian, south of Edinburgh, also called Rosslyn. This small village has become world famous for two quite distinct reasons: Rosslyn Chapel and the Roslin Institute. The 15th-century Rosslyn Chapel was built by the Sinclair family and is one of the most remarkable buildings in Scotland, with intricate architecture and links to the Knights Templar and the Holy Grail legend, brought to global prominence by Dan Brown's book *The Da Vinci Code*. The Roslin Institute is a world leader in animal research and in 1997 announced the successful cloning of Dolly the Sheep (named after American country singer Dolly Parton, as she was cloned from a sheep's mammary gland).

It has been said that the names 'Roslin' and 'Rosslyn' derive from the 'Rose Line', either in reference to the Paris Meridian (a rival to the Greenwich Meridian in London as the centre of world longitude) or to the theory of the blood-line of Jesus and Mary Magdalene, as espoused in several bestselling books. However, the name does not refer to the descendants of Christ living in Midlothian, but originates from the Brythonic *ros* meaning 'promontory' (or perhaps *rhos* meaning 'meadow') and *celyn* meaning 'holly', therefore giving us 'holly point' or 'holly meadow'.

Other famous Roslins include television presenter Gaby Roslin.

Ross

Area of the Highlands, stretching from the east coast to the west coast of the Scottish mainland. Ross was part of the former county of Ross and Cromarty and before that (as Ross-shire) a county in its own right. Ross is often divided into Easter Ross and Wester Ross, with Wester Ross containing many of Scotland's most stunning coastal locations, including Lochcarron, Applecross, Torridon, and Ullapool. The name 'Ross' derives from the Gaelic word *ros* meaning 'headland' or 'promontory'.

Ross also gave its name to the Clan Ross, the surname Ross, and the male personal name Ross, so giving the world singer Diana Ross, chat-show host Jonathan Ross, and Ross Geller from the sitcom *Friends*.

Rosyth

Town in Fife. Rosyth is known for the naval base and dockyard that has been based there since 1909. The town was built around the site of the ruined 15th-century Rosyth Castle, and the name derives from the Gaelic word *ros* meaning 'headland' or 'promontory', although it is unclear what the second syllable means.

Rothesay

Main town on the Isle of Bute. Rothesay was for many years popular with Glaswegians, who would go 'doon the watter' (down the Firth of Clyde) to spend their summer holidays there. The town has long been associated with the Stewarts (known in Bute as the Stuarts), and from the 14th century the heir to the Scottish throne was given the title of Duke of Rothesay. The ruined Rothesay Castle was also a residence of the Stewart kings. The title of Duke of Rothesay survived both the Union of the Crowns and the fall of the Stewarts, and is still used by the heir to the British crown, with Prince Charles being the current Duke. The name 'Rothesay' derives from the Norse, with *Rotha* being a personal name and *ey* meaning 'island'.

Roxburgh

Village in the Borders. Roxburgh was once one of the most important towns in Scotland, before being destroyed in 1460, and gave its name to the former county of Roxburghshire. The name comes from the Old English *hroc* (either meaning 'rook' or a personal name) and *burgh* (meaning 'town'). The title of Duke of Roxburghe takes its name from the place. Roxburgh is also a Scottish surname, and famous Roxburghs include former Scotland football manager Andy Roxburgh.

Royal Mile

Historic street in Edinburgh. The Royal Mile is arguably the most famous street in Scotland and runs from Edinburgh Castle in the west to the Palace of Holyroodhouse in the east. The Royal Mile was so named as the distance between the Castle and the Palace was a Scottish mile (the equivalent of 1.1 English miles or 1.8 kilometres), with the 'Royal' epithet being added in recognition of David I, who began the building of the street in the 12th century.

Confusingly for visitors, the street is not officially called 'The Royal Mile', but rather 'The High Street'. Even more confusingly, 'The High Street' is the official name of only one section of the Royal Mile, with other sections including the Castle Esplanade, Castlehill, Lawnmarket, Canongate, and Abbey Strand.

As well as the Castle and the Palace of Holyrood, the Royal Mile includes some of Edinburgh's most famous buildings, including St Giles' Cathedral, the John Knox House, Scotland's High Court and Court of Session, and the new Scottish Parliament at Holyrood.

The Royal Mile is also said to be one of the most haunted areas not merely in Scotland, but in the whole world, and there are many tours that take tourists along or underneath the Royal Mile in search of strange or unexplained phenomena – or failing that, people dressed up as ghosts who will jump out and try and scare you.

Rum

Largest of the Small Isles in the Inner Hebrides. The island is known for its flora and fauna and is managed by Scottish National Heritage as a National Nature Reserve. The name 'Rum' is of uncertain origin, although it probably means 'wide' or 'spacious' (either from the Gaelic word *rum* meaning 'spacious', or from the Norse *rom ey* meaning 'wide island').

There is sadly no connection between the island of Rum and the alcoholic drink of the same name, and attempts were made to differentiate the two by changing the spelling of the island to 'Rhum', although 'Rum' remains the official name.

Rutherglen

Suburb of Glasgow, in South Lanarkshire. Rutherglen was formerly an important industrial town and historic royal burgh, and actor Robbie Coltrane was born there. The name 'Rutherglen' comes from the Gaelic name *Ruardhgleann* meaning 'red valley' or 'red glen'.

St Andrews

Seaside town in Fife. St Andrews is home to the oldest university in Scotland, established in 1411, and the most famous golf course in the world, often called 'the Home of Golf'. The town became famous from the 9th century onwards as an important Scottish religious centre, having been established in honour of Saint Andrew, a disciple of Jesus and brother of Peter, whose bones were believed to have been taken from Constantinople and buried in Fife. It was also said that Saint Andrew was crucified on a diagonal cross rather than a standard cross, which gave us the Saint Andrew's Cross that became the basis of the Scottish flag. Saint Andrew became the patron saint of Scotland, as well as of Greece and Russia (who presumably also have some of his bones), and his feast day is November 30th.

The 12th century St Andrew's Cathedral, which was at the time the largest building in Scotland, fell into decay in the 17th century, but is still a popular tourist destination. The Royal and Ancient Golf Course was founded in the 19th century and has hosted the Open Golf Championship 28 times, more than any other course. The University of St Andrews remains one of the most prestigious universities in the world, with a certain couple known as William Wales and Katherine Middleton being recent alumni. However St Andrews still does not have a railway station, with the nearest one being at Leuchars, some six miles away.

St Kilda

Island archipelago 40 miles west of the Outer Hebrides. St Kilda is known as one of Scotland's most famous uninhabited islands, although it is in fact the name for the island group and not the main island. (The main island, which was inhabited for around 2000 years, was called Hirta.) The St Kildans were the most isolated community in Scotland and the final 36 islanders were finally evacuated, at their own request, in 1930. St Kilda is today the location of a defence installation, and is owned by the National Trust of Scotland and has been designated a World Heritage Site.

There has been much discussion of the origin of the name 'St Kilda', as there is no saint called Kilda or anything similar. The name has been used since the 16th century and is believed to have been a misprint by Dutch cartographers for the Norse *skildir* (meaning 'shields', in reference to the shape of the islands) or *Skaldar* (the Norse name for the uninhabited Haskeir Island, which lies between St Kilda and the Outer Hebrides and was wrongly associated with the islands). Another theory is that St Kilda takes its name from the spring called *Childa* on *Hirta*, wrongly thought to

have been a holy well and therefore called 'St Kilda'.
The archipelago is often known as 'The Islands on
the Edge of the World' after the book and film of that
name – although the 1936 Michael Powell film was
not filmed on St Kilda, but on the remote Shetland
island of Foula.

St Kilda is also the name of a popular seaside suburb
of Melbourne, home to an Australian Rules Football
team. The Melbourne St Kilda is considerably warmer
than its North Atlantic counterpart.

Sauchiehall Street

Famous street in Glasgow. Sauchiehall Street is
known for its shopping, cinemas, and tea-rooms, and
often shortened to simply 'Sauchie'. Although it is
associated with the centre of Glasgow, the street is
over 1.5 miles long and runs from Buchanan Street
in the east to Kelvingrove in the west. Sauchiehall
Street was originally a long narrow lane surrounded
by large houses and gardens, and the name actually
derives from *Sauchiehaugh*, with *saugh* the Scots word
for 'willow' (deriving from the Gaelic *saileach*) and
haugh the Scots word for 'meadow in a river valley' –
a word that would later be corrupted to the English
word 'hall'.

Scalloway

Fishing port on the west coast of the Mainland of Shetland and former capital of the islands. The name 'Scalloway' derives from the Norse *skali* meaning 'huts' or 'house' and *vagr* meaning 'bay'.

Scapa Flow

Large area of sheltered seawater almost enclosed by the islands of Orkney. Scapa Flow's position as a very large natural harbour was utilized in both World Wars as it became the main base for the British Navy. The most famous event to occur at Scapa Flow, however, took place in 1919, a year after the end of the First World War. The defeated German Navy, whose ships had been taken to Scapa Flow until a decision was made about what to do with them, deliberately scuttled 51 vessels in the greatest loss of shipping ever to take place at one time.

The name 'Scapa Flow' comes from the Norse name *Skalpeid Floi* meaning 'bay of the long valley isthmus'.

Scone

Small town near Perth. One of the most historic locations in Scotland, Scone was the ancient capital of Alba (the Gaelic kingdom of the Scots and the Picts) from the 9th century to the 11th century, and was the ceremonial coronation site for Scotland's monarchs from Kenneth MacAlpine in the 9th century until James I of Scotland in 1424. In 1651, during the protectorate of Oliver Cromwell, Charles II was crowned King of Scotland at Scone, but had to wait until 1660 before the Restoration of the monarchy was finally complete.

The most precious symbol of the coronation – and of Scotland itself – is the Stone of Destiny (also called the Stone of Scone), a block of sandstone that is said to have been the stone that Jacob slept on in *The Book of Genesis*. The Stone was removed from Scone to Westminster Abbey by Edward I in 1297, and remained there until 1996, when it was returned to Scotland. It is currently on display at Edinburgh Castle (assuming that it is the real Stone and not, as conspiracy theorists have suggested, a copy).

Scone Palace, which still stands today, was built on the site of a former abbey and royal residence by the Earls of Mansfield in the 19th century.

The name 'Scone' derives from the Gaelic *sgonn* and means 'mound'. It is pronounced 'skoon', as opposed to the delicious Scottish cake enjoyed with butter, jam, or cream, which derives from the Gaelic *scon* meaning 'flat' and is pronounced 'skon' or (in refined company) 'skone'.

Selkirk

Historic town in the Borders and former county town of Selkirkshire. People from Selkirk are called 'Souters' due to the town's traditional association with shoemaking. Sir Walter Scott was Sheriff in Selkirk, and the *Selkirk Grace* is a verse attributed to Robert Burns and associated with Burns Night. The town's name derives from the Old English *Seles Chirche* meaning 'church in the forest', with the 'church' being changed to the Scots form *kirk*.

Selkirk is also a surname, and famous Selkirks include Scottish castaway Alexander Selkirk, who was the inspiration behind the novel *Robinson Crusoe*.

Shetland

Group of around 100 islands (around 20 inhabited) off the north coast of Scotland. Shetland is the most northerly part of the United Kingdom, 60 miles north of Orkney, and the nearest city is Bergen in Norway. Shetland is famous for its historic archaeology with sites dating back to the Bronze Age. Shetland was ruled by Norway from the 9th century until 1469 when it was ceded to Scotland, but it still commemorates this heritage in the annual Viking festival called Up-Helly-Aa.

Shetland is a major fishing region and from the

1970s onwards became the centre of the North Sea Oil industry, with Britain's largest oil terminal based at Sullom Voe. People from Shetland are called Shetlanders and speak a distinctive dialect partly derived from the Norn language, Shetland's variation of Norse, which was spoken until the 19th century. Famous Shetlanders include former Chancellor of the Exchequer Norman Lamont.

The name 'Shetland' derives from the Norse name *Hjaltland* which means 'hilt land', the hilt referring to the dagger-like shape of the islands. The opening letters 'hj' were replaced with 'sh' and 'Hjaltland' became 'Shetland' (although, with Scots gradually replacing Norn, Shetland gained an alternative English name of 'Zetland', which was the official name of the local council until it reverted to Shetland in 1975).

Shetland is famous for its birdlife and knitwear, and also gives its name to several unique animals: the small and popular Shetland pony, the small dog breed called the Shetland sheepdog (which also goes by the name of 'sheltie'), and a small breed of sheep called the Shetland, which is known for its fine wool. The people of Shetland, however, are mainly of normal height.

Shettleston

Area in the east end of Glasgow. Shettleston is, sadly, best known for having one of the lowest life expectancies in Britain. The name comes from the 12th-century *Shedilstoune* and possibly derives from an Irish female personal name *Seadna*.

Shiel

Name of a loch, glen, and river in the Highlands. Loch Shiel is a freshwater loch in Lochaber and was crossed in 1745 by Bonnie Prince Charlie before he raised the Jacobite standard at Glenfinnan. The unconnected Glen Shiel is to be found further north in Lochalsh, and is a popular destination for hill-walkers, with seven Munros on the Glen Shiel Ridge. The origin of the name is unknown, but it has been suggested that it might be an old Brythonic or Pictish word for 'flowing'. Glen Shiel was the site of the only battle of short-lived and often-forgotten 1719 Jacobite rising, with the Jacobites being easily defeated as usual.

Shotts

Former mining town in North Lanarkshire near Motherwell. The name probably derives from the Gaelic *Sceots* meaning 'steep slopes'.

Skara Brae

Neolithic settlement on the west coast of the Mainland of Orkney. The site dates back to 3000BC and is thought to be the oldest human settlement in Britain. The settlement had been undiscovered for thousands of years until a severe storm in 1850 disturbed a large mound that was known locally as Skerrabra. The site is now a World Heritage Site and popular tourist destination, with the name changed to Skara Brae. *Brae* is the Scots word for 'hill' or 'slope', although the original name *Skerrabra* might possibly derive from the Norse world *sker* meaning 'rock in the sea', a word that is anglicized as 'skerry'.

Skye

Largest island in the Inner Hebrides. Skye is Scotland's second-largest island after the island of Lewis and Harris, and is known for its spectacular scenery, including the magnificent mountains of the Cuillins, and for the 'Skye Boat Song', which tells of Bonnie Prince Charlie's escape to the island after his defeat at Culloden. Anybody fleeing to Skye today would do better to take the Skye Bridge, which was opened in 1995.

The Gaelic name for Skye is *An t-Eilean Sgitheanach*, which means 'winged island', and the Norse name was *Skuyo*, meaning 'island of mist'. Skye has in recent years become a popular Scottish girls' name.

A Skye Terrier is a small breed of dog with a long fringe, which was first bred on the island. The most famous Skye Terrier was Greyfriars' Bobby from

Edinburgh, who faithfully stayed at the graveside of his master for 14 years and has been the subject of several books and films.

Solway Firth

Area of sea that separates south-west Scotland from north-west England and stretches to the Mull of Galloway in the west. The name 'Solway' is the anglicized form of the Norse *sol vath* meaning 'muddy ford', with 'Firth' being the Scots form of the Norse *fjordr* meaning 'inland sea' or 'estuary'.

Spey

Second-longest river in Scotland. The Spey is renowned for both salmon fishing and the production of whisky. As with most of Scotland's great rivers, the derivation of the name is lost in time. It has been suggested that it might be of Brythonic origin and mean either 'gushing' – the Spey is the fastest flowing river in Scotland – or 'hawthorn'.

Speyside (or Strathspey) is the area around the valley of the River Spey and is popular both for tourism and as for being the site of half of the whisky distilleries in Scotland (and home of many of Scotland's most famous and distinctive single malts, such as Glenfiddich, Glenlivet, and Macallan).

Springburn

North-eastern suburb of Glasgow. Springburn developed in the 19th century through the railway industry and was at one point one of the biggest manufacturers of trains in the world. The origin of the name is unclear, but is believed to derive literally from a spring and a burn.

Staffa

Uninhabited island in the Inner Hebrides west of Mull. Staffa is famous for its large hexagonal columns or pillars of basalt, the best known being the large sea cave called Fingal's Cave after the Celtic hero Fingal. This became even better known as a result of the *Hebrides Overture* (also known as *Fingal's Cave*) by Felix Mendelssohn, who was inspired by his visit to Staffa in 1829. The name 'Staffa' derives from the Norse *stafr ey* and appropriately means 'island of pillars'.

Stenhousemuir

Town near Falkirk. Stenhousemuir that takes its name from the Old English *stan hus* meaning 'stone house', with *muir*, the Scots word for 'moor' being added later on.

Stirling

City and local-government authority in central Scotland. Stirling was one of Scotland's first royal burghs and achieved the status of a city in 2002. In medieval times it was Scotland's most important military garrison. William Wallace won a famous battle against the English at Stirling Bridge in 1297, and the 1314 Battle of Bannockburn took place nearby. Stirling boasts a historic castle, dating from the 16th century, and a modern university founded in 1967.

The meaning of the name 'Stirling' is unclear, but it possibly comes from an old Gaelic phrase meaning 'enclosed land by the stream'.

Famous people born in Stirling include former Scotland football captain Billy Bremner. Another sporting legend nominally associated with Stirling is motor-racing driver Stirling Moss, whose name became synonymous with fast driving, so that for decades anybody who was cautioned for speeding would be asked, 'Who do you think you are? Stirling Moss?'

Stonehaven

Historic town south of Aberdeen. Stonehaven was formerly a major fishing port and is famous for being the location of the Hogmanay Fireballs Festival and for being the nearest town to Dunnottar Castle. Famous people born in Stonehaven include the first Director-General of the BBC, John Reith. The name 'Stonehaven' is not actually thought to mean 'stone haven'. The town was originally called 'Stonehive', with *hive* possibly deriving from an Old English word *hyth* meaning 'landing place'.

Stornoway

Town on the island of Lewis and Harris. Stornoway is the largest town in the Hebrides and administrative centre of the Na-hEileanan Siar local-government authority. The Gaelic name for Stornoway is *Steornabhagh*, and the town is known for being predominantly Gaelic-speaking and for its strong Presbyterianism and adherence to the Sabbath.

Famous people born in Stornoway include Canadian explorer Alexander MacKenzie. Stornoway was built around a natural harbour and the name derives from the Norse *Stjornavagar* meaning 'steering bay'.

Stranraer

Town and port in south-west Scotland. Stranraer is best known for its ferry link to Northern Ireland. The name derives from the Gaelic *sron reamhar* meaning either 'fat nose' or more prosaically 'broad peninsula'.

Strathaven

Small town near Hamilton in South Lanarkshire. The name 'Strathaven' means 'wide valley of the Avon' with the Avon being the Avon Water, whose name derives from the Gaelic *abhainn* meaning 'river'. It was near Strathaven that Rudolf Hess bailed out in 1941 in his still-unexplained attempt to visit the Duke of Hamilton in the middle of the Second World War. The name of the town is locally pronounced 'stray-ven', with the letters 'ath' not sounded.

Strathclyde

Area in south-west Scotland. Strathclyde was an ancient kingdom of the Britons that arose in the 5th century with Dumbarton as its capital. Strathclyde's power was seriously diminished by Viking attacks in the 9th century and the kingdom became increasingly aligned with the Scottish kingdom of Dalriada (later to became Alba), before finally being incorporated into the Scottish nation in the 11th century. The Britons, however, left a permanent mark on the west of Scotland with their Brythonic language, more akin to Welsh than to Gaelic, which is the root of many historic place names, such as Glasgow, Paisley, and the Clyde itself.

Strathclyde was resurrected in 1975 as the name

of Scotland's most populous local-government region, including Glasgow, Ayrshire, Lanarkshire, Renfrewshire, Dunbartonshire, and Argyll, although the region was broken up in the reforms of 1996. Strathclyde University is one of Glasgow's four universities and was founded in 1964.

The name 'Strathclyde' means 'wide valley of the Clyde', with *strath* meaning 'wide valley' in Gaelic.

Strathdon

Area in Aberdeenshire. The name 'Strathdon' means 'wide valley of the River Don'. The name is also given to a local village, which was formerly known as Invernochty, as it was located where the Water of Nochty met the Don.

Strathmore

Valley in Angus and Perth and Kinross. The name means 'great wide valley', with *mor* being Gaelic for 'great' or 'big', and the valley of Strathmore certainly contains some of the best arable land in Scotland. The title of Earl of Strathmore has been in the Lyon family since the 17th century, with the family seat at Glamis Castle.

Strathspey

Area in north-east Scotland. Strathspey ('the wide valley of the Spey') is another name for Speyside, the area with Grantown-on-Spey as its main town that includes many of Scotland's most famous whisky distilleries.

The strathspey is also a Scottish country dance with a slower tempo than the more energetic jigs and reels, which thus allows the more exuberant dancers to take a break and repair to the bar.

Stromness

Second-largest town in Orkney. Stromness is a ferry port and destination for services from the Scottish mainland. The town takes its name from the Norse *straumr* meaning 'currents' or 'tides' and *nes* meaning 'headland'. Famous people from Stromness include the writer George Mackay Brown.

Stromness is also the name of the whaling station on the island of South Georgia that was the destination in 1916 for Ernest Shackleton's epic journey to raise help to save his stranded crewmates in Antarctica.

Sutherland

Area of the northern Highlands and formerly a local-government authority. Sutherland is now best known for the Sutherland Clearances of the 19th century, when the Countess of Sutherland forcibly moved tenants off her estates to make room for sheep. The name of the area comes from the Norse *suthr land* meaning 'southern land', for although the area stands at the very north of the Scottish mainland, it was at the very south of the Viking-controlled territory governed for Norway by the Earl of Orkney.

Sutherland would become a clan name and a popular Scottish surname. Famous Sutherlands include Canadian film actor Donald Sutherland and his son Kiefer Sutherland, star of television series *24*.

Tain

Historic town in Easter Ross. The name of the town derives from the small river called the Tain Water, whose origin, as with many rivers, is uncertain but probably comes from ancient Brythonic. It may simply mean 'water'.

Tarbert

Name of many places in Scotland. The name 'Tarbert' (sometimes found in the form 'Tarbat') derives from the Gaelic *tairbeart* meaning 'isthmus' or 'portage point' (with 'portage' being the term for dragging boats across a narrow strip of land between two areas of water).

The more noteworthy Tarberts in Scotland include the main settlement on Harris and a fishing village at the narrowest point of the Kintyre peninsula.

Tay

Longest river in Scotland. The River Tay flows from Loch Tay in Perthshire through both Perth and Dundee into the Firth of Tay. The Tay is famous for salmon and trout fishing and infamous for the Tay Bridge Disaster of 1879 when the bridge over the river collapsed and 75 lives were lost. A replacement bridge was completed in 1888. The disaster was commemorated in a memorably bad poem by William McGonagal, which featured the famous lines:

And the cry rang out all round the toun
Good heavens! The Tay Bridge has blown down.

Tayside is the area around the River Tay and was the name of a former council region. The meaning of 'Tay' is ancient and unclear, but probably of Brythonic origin meaning 'strong' or 'flowing'.

Thurso

Town on the north coast of Caithness. Thurso is the nearest town to the now-decommissioned Dounreay nuclear plant. The name 'Thurso' derives from the Norse *thjors aa* and means 'bull's water'.

Tiree

Island in the Inner Hebrides. Tiree is a picturesque and highly fertile island, the latter aspect of its nature being expressed in its name, which comes from the Gaelic *tir eadha* and means 'land of corn'.

Tobermory

Main town on the island of Mull. Tobermory is famous for its colourful buildings, which were used as the location for the children's television series *Balamory*. The town also appears indirectly in another popular children's television series with Tobermory being the name of one of the characters in *The Wombles*. The name 'Tobermory' derives from the Gaelic name *Tobar Moire* meaning 'Mary's well', referring not to the health of a local resident, but to a well that was dedicated to the Virgin Mary.

Tomintoul

Village in Moray. At over 1100 feet, Tomintoul is said to be the highest village in the Highlands. The name derives from the Gaelic *tom an t-Sabhail* meaning 'hillock of the barn'.

Torridon

Scenic region of Wester Ross and also the name of a sea loch. The origin of the name 'Torridon' is unclear. The first part comes from *torr*, the Gaelic word for 'hill', but there is no agreement on where the *idon* comes from.

Troon

Coastal town in South Ayrshire. Troon is famous as a holiday resort and for being the location of one Scotland's best known golf courses, which has hosted the Open Championship eight times. The name 'Troon' derives either from the Brythonic *trwyn* meaning 'headland' or from the Gaelic name *An t-Sron* meaning 'the nose', because of its appearance on the map (as compared to Stranraer, further down the coast, whose name in Gaelic means the less complimentary 'the fat nose').

Trossachs

Area in Stirling between Loch Lomond and Callander. The Trossachs is known for its picturesque scenery and is part of the Loch Lomond and Trossachs National Park. The novels of Sir Walter Scott made this area a popular tourist destination, and the outlaw Rob Roy Macgregor lived in the area. The origin of the word

'Trossachs' is unclear, but it is probably Brythonic and might mean 'cross-hills'.

Tweed

River in the Borders. The Tweed flows through Peebles, Kelso, and Selkirk before reaching the sea at Berwick-upon-Tweed. The river is famous for its salmon fishing and also gives its name to the luxury cloth favoured by those who partake of outdoor activities. The origin of the name 'Tweed' is unknown, but (as with the name of the River Tay) it might possibly derive from the Brythonic word *tau* meaning 'flowing'. The use of the name for cloth was apparently a misprint, as the original word for the woven cloth was 'tweel', but when some Border tweels were sold to London in the 19th century, they were mistakenly thought to have been called 'tweeds'. The name was never changed back.

Tweeddale is the name of the historic district around the upper reaches of the River Tweed, and its boundaries broadly correspond with those of the former county of Peeblesshire. The word 'dale' is an English word meaning 'valley', which is found elsewhere in southern Scotland in place names such as Annandale and Clydesdale.

Uddingston

Small town in South Lanarkshire. The name
'Uddingston' possibly derives from an Old English or
Norse personal name *Oda*, with the name meaning
'the town of Oda's people'. Uddingston is famous
for being the home of the Tunnock's confectionery
company – world renowned as the maker of
magnificent tea cakes and caramel wafers.

Uist

Name of two large Hebridean Islands, North Uist and
South Uist. South Uist has a slightly larger population
and area than North Uist and is predominantly
Catholic, while North Uist is predominantly
Presbyterian. The islands are not adjoining, as the
island of Benbecula sits between them. The name
'Uist' derives from the Norse *inni-vist* and means 'a
dwelling' or 'an abode'. Famous people from the Uists
include national heroine Flora Macdonald, who was
born in South Uist.

Ullapool

Town in Wester Ross. Ullapool was founded as a
herring port in 1788 and was designed by Thomas
Telford. It has become a tourist centre and is also a
departure point for ferries to Stornoway. Contrary

to expectation, the name does not refer to the town's harbour but derives from the Norse *Olaf bolstadr* meaning 'Olaf's farmstead'. This was shortened over time to *Olaf bol* and then anglicized to 'Ullapool'.

Wanlockhead

Village in Dumfries and Galloway. Wanlockhead is one of the highest villages in Scotland and was for centuries (along with the nearby village of Leadhills) known for mining. Lead, silver, and gold were all mined nearby, and Wanlockhead gained the nickname of 'God's Treasure House'. The village was previously known as Winlocke and the name possibly derives from the Gaelic *cuingealach* meaning 'narrow place', with *head* added later in reference to the village's position at the head of the stream Wanlock Water.

Waverley

Main railway station of Edinburgh. It was opened in the 1840s and takes its name from the famous series of novels by Sir Walter Scott that included *Rob Roy* and *Ivanhoe*. The first of the series was *Waverley* itself, first published in 1814, the story of an English soldier called Edward Waverley who is sent to Scotland during the 1745 rebellion and ends up fighting for the Jacobites.

Wemyss

Names of two places in Scotland. In the east, the area of Wemyss along the Fife coast includes Wemyss Castle, which dates back to the 15th century. In the west, Wemyss Bay is a Victorian village on the Firth of Clyde from where a ferry service runs to Rothesay on the Isle of Bute. The name 'Wemyss' is pronounced 'weemz' and derives from the Gaelic word *uaimh* meaning 'caves' (which you will find in both areas).

West Lothian

Local-government area to the west of Edinburgh. It is (with Midlothian and East Lothian) one of the three divisions of the ancient kingdom of Lothian. West Lothian is also famous for the 'West Lothian question'. This refers to a parliamentary question first asked in 1977 by the then Member of Parliament for West Lothian (later for Linlithgow), Tam Dalyell, who pointed out a problem associated with the devolving powers to a Scottish Parliament, saying:

> *For how long will English constituencies and English MPs tolerate MPs from Scotland exercising an important, and probably often decisive, effect on British politics while they themselves have no say in the same matters in Scotland?*

To this date, and despite the creation of the Holyrood

Parliament in 1999, no one has been able to give a satisfactory answer to Mr Dalyell's question.

Whalsay

Island in the Shetland group. Whalsay lies to the east of the Mainland and has recently become the second-largest of the Shetland Islands by population. It is a major fishing community and also boasts the most northerly eighteen-hole golf course in Britain. The name 'Whalsay' is derived from the Norse name *Hvalsey* and means 'whale island' – and if you are lucky you might be able to see whales around the Whalsay coast.

Whithorn

Small town in Galloway. Whithorn is best known for being the location of the first Christian church in Scotland (or at least the first Christian church that we know of), and can lay a plausible claim to being the oldest surviving Scottish town. Saint Ninian is credited with founding a church there around AD400, and this is recorded in Latin as being called *Candida Casa*, which means 'the white house'. This name was then translated into Old English as *hwit erne*, which later became 'Whithorn'.

The nearby fishing village of Isle of Whithorn is

actually no longer an island, as a causeway was built to connect it to the mainland in the 1790s.

Wick

Town on the north-west coast of the Scottish mainland. Wick was the county town of the former county of Caithness and for a period in the 19th century was the centre of the Scottish herring industry. The name 'Wick' derives from the Norse word *vik* and means 'bay'.

Wigtown

Small town in south-west Scotland. Wigtown gave its name to the former county of Wigtownshire and has recently been designated as Scotland's National Book Town, with a book festival and numerous bookshops. There is also a place called Wigton in Cumbria, and both names are believed to derive from an English person called Wigca.

Wishaw

Town in Lanarkshire. Wishaw was formerly at the centre of coal, iron, and steel industries. The meaning of 'Wishaw' is unclear with the *shaw* part being the Scots word for 'wood', but there being no definitive answer as to what the *wi* represents.

Yell

Second-largest island in Shetland by area. Although the wind may blow fiercely there, the name 'Yell' does not have any connections with raised voices, but is derived from the Norse *geldr* meaning 'barren'. Sure enough, two-thirds of the island is covered in peat.

Suggestions for Further Reading

The Scottish Islands: Hamish Haswell-Smith (Canongate)

Tracing Your Scottish Ancestors: Cecil Sinclair (Mercat Press)

Oxford Dictionary of First Names: Patrick Hanks & Flavia Hodges (OUP)

Scottish Place Names: WFH Nicolaisen(Batsford)

Scottish Place Names: David Ross (Birlinn)

Scottish Surnames: George Mackay (Lomond Books)

Bumper Book Of Babies Names: Jacqueline Harrod & Andre Page (Clarion)

Collins Guide to Scots Kith & Kin (Harper Collins)

Scottish Surnames: David Dorward (Mercat Press)

Scotland's Place Names: David Dorward (Mercat Press)

Clans & Tartans: James MacKay (Lomond Books)

Scottish First Names: George MacKay (Lomond Books)

Scottish Christian Names: Leslie Alan Dunkling (Johnson & Bacon)

Illustrated Encyclopedia of Scotland: edited Iseabail MacLeod (Lomond Books)

Collins Encyclopedia of Scotland: John & Julia Keay (Harper Collins)

Surnames of Scotland: George F. Black (Birlinn)

Scottish Names (Harper Collins)

Scottish Words (Harper Collins)